UNDERSTANDING
FAMILY SUPPORT

UNDERSTANDING FAMILY SUPPORT

POLICY, PRACTICE AND THEORY

JOHN CANAVAN, JOHN PINKERTON AND PAT DOLAN

Jessica Kingsley *Publishers*
London and Philadelphia

First published in 2016
by Jessica Kingsley *Publishers*
73 Collier Street
London N1 9BE, UK
and
400 Market Street, Suite 400
Philadelphia, PA 19106, USA

www.jkp.com

Library of Congress Cataloging in Publication Data
Names: Canavan, John, 1967- author. | Pinkerton, John, 1953- author. | Dolan, Pat, 1958- author.
Title: Understanding family support : policy, practice and theory / John Canavan, John Pinkerton and Pat Dolan.
Description: London ; Philadelphia : Jessica Kingsley Publishers, 2016. | Includes bibliographical references.
Identifiers: LCCN 2015046782 | ISBN 9781849050661 (alk. paper)
Subjects: LCSH: Family services. | Family social work.
Classification: LCC HV697 .C36 2016 | DDC 362.82/8--dc23 LC record available at
http://lccn.loc.gov/2015046782

British Library Cataloguing in Publication Data
A CIP catalogue record for this book is available from the British Library

ISBN 978 1 84905 066 1
eISBN 978 0 85700 258 7

Printed and bound in Great Britain

MIX
Paper from
responsible sources
FSC® C013056

CONTENTS

Chapter One

INTRODUCTION

TAKING A POSITION ON FAMILY SUPPORT

INTRODUCTION

Over the last two decades family support has gained – and, despite some waxing and waning in influence, maintained – a place among the key organising concepts for the development and implementation of child welfare policy and practice in a range of countries. Building on a history that in the UK can be traced back to the nineteenth century (Frost, Abbott and Race 2015), the family support literature now provides a rich and international pool of experience and understanding (Canavan, Dolan and Pinkerton 2000; Daly *et al.* 2015; Dolan, Pinkerton and Canavan 2006; Featherstone 2006; Featherstone, White and Morris 2014; Frost *et al.* 2015; Katz and Pinkerton 2003a; Statham and Smith 2010). One explanation for the usefulness and longevity of family support as a concept has been its range and flexibility – acting as a policy direction, a set of characteristics for service development, a style of practice and an area of research. However, that range and flexibility has also been its major weakness. To date, family support has lacked sufficient theoretical, empirical and programmatic coherence to set the child welfare agenda. Rather, the concept has been used as a means of articulating aspects of more or less compatible policy and practice – a role it has played alongside, and at times in competition with, the concepts of prevention and early intervention. Family support as a shared term has also acted as a cover for different aspirations expressed through apparently similar approaches to child welfare that are actually significantly different in orientation – the remedial, the protective and the developmental.

The basic argument of this book is that if family support is to become the defining child welfare paradigm, it is crucial for its supporters to develop a single, strong synthesising position on what it means and why. This attempt to clearly set out the core contents and parameters of a paradigm of practice is challenging and will no doubt be contested from a range of perspectives. It is important to stress that what is being attempted here is not the aim of narrowing the concept of family support, to limit its expression in diverse practices, nor to quash debate. Rather, through stating explicit positions on what family support needs to be, the intention is to make those positions more open to examination and contest – not just as ideas, but in practice. Taking and articulating clear positions will provide a firmer basis for the work of those practitioners (and that includes researchers, policy-makers, trainers and managers, as well as those directly delivering services) who are committed to family support as a critical, reflective, empowering practice.

In this chapter, five clear positions are taken. The first is on reflective practice as the epistemological foundation for developing an understanding of family support. The second is on the major theories that are needed to frame and inform family support – social ecology, resilience, social support and social capital. A third position is taken on the core nature of family support presented as a definition. This is then followed by identifying, as a fourth position, the core components of any family support intervention. The fifth foundational position relates to the style of practice that family support must encompass, presented in a set of ten essential practice principles. Having stated the five positions that mark out the foundations of the book, this chapter ends by setting out the contents of the five chapters to follow.

FAMILY SUPPORT AS REFLECTIVE PRACTICE

Involvement in the field of family support constantly throws up the challenge of finding ways to articulate what it is that is being offered to families, why it is being offered, and how it will contribute to meeting the needs and realising the rights of both parents and children. This is often posed as a question of outcomes, and all too often family support is pitted against child protection – in policy and research debate as well as in questioning frontline service delivery. Every situation requires its own specific explanation, but family support practitioners, whether managing or delivering services, advising a politician on policy or designing a research project, need to be confident that what they are doing has meaning and significance for improving the lives of those they seek to support, both children and parents within families. This confidence can only come from constantly engaging in questioning individual actions and the structural constraints and opportunities that frame those actions. This requires a mixture of description and questioning informed by action leading to change, which provides the basis for reflective practice.

There is an extensive literature on reflective practice based on the learning cycle of experience – observation and reflection – and the development of concepts – the testing of concepts in practice (Knott and Scragg 2010). This experiential learning can be achieved by both 'reflection on action' and 'reflection in action'. The first starts with recalling a past incident, describing it, analysing what happened, and then evaluating and learning lessons for the future from the process of reflection (Dolan *et al.* 2006, pp.17/18). The second involves similarly processing experience, but doing so as part of the experience itself in order to enhance understanding and effectiveness in the present. Both modes are a response to complexity: 'the indeterminate swampy zones of practice involving uncertainty, uniqueness and value conflict' (Schon, cited in Knott and Scragg 2010, p.7).

For reflective practice it is that lived experience that is privileged as the raw material for the structured, systematic reflective processes from which family support practice improvement and improvement in the lives of families can emerge (Canavan *et al.* 2009). At the same time, reflection needs to be theoretically framed if it is to be effectively analysed:

> ...the idea of lens here may be helpful in trying to understand the experience being reflected upon. What frame of reference (or lens) is being used to make sense of what has happened? What theories are being applied to this situation? It is easy to reinforce previously held opinions about people and situations which may lead to prejudice and discriminatory practice if we do not recognise what we are using to make sense of reflections... When someone who wears glasses puts them on, the difference in being able to see clearly is immense. Things come into focus and clear patterns emerge. (Knott and Scragg 2010, p.6)

While commitment to reflective practice is the cornerstone position for family support, it is important to note that it is not without its difficulties and its critics (Wilson 2013). Reflective practice has also been criticised for being too individualised, with insufficient attention to organisational and structural constraints. According to Adams (2009), a critical approach is required because, at best, practitioners find optimal ways of working within the constraints or, at worst, they accommodate them. Concern has also been expressed that reflective practice is not sufficiently individualised in that attention is only given to reflecting on the conscious, whereas an adequate understanding of experience also needs to address the unconscious (Ruch, Turney and Ward 2010). Another obvious risk is that external knowledge from theory and empirical research is given less priority in the learning cycle than the immediacy of the contingencies and emotional content of practice. Indeed, for some, the 'professional artistry' (Knott and Scragg 2010, p.7) of reflection in action has been counterposed to the scientific theory development and technical application of evidence-based practice, with its 'functionalist and technocratic underpinnings of competence-based learning' (Wilson 2013, p.156). Such a divide is not necessary, as within the field of reflective practice there are various modes of reflection beyond the basic two of reflection on and in action (Ruch 2007):

- Practical reflection: seeing knowledge acquisition as having a 'bottom-up', 'from practice' focus.

- Critical reflection: focusing on emancipatory sources of knowledge, involving challenges to existing social conditions and structural forces that distort practice.

- Technical reflection: linked to instrumental, problem-solving, reflecting and privileging expert and external sources of knowledge.

- Process reflection: focusing on the conscious and unconscious aspects of practice and recognising the impact of the emotional content of the work.

The challenge is not to privilege one over the other, but to keep them all in play. Reflective practice needs to encompass each of the four modes in order to allow for the incorporation of individual and social levels of analysis, and objective and subjective sources of data, while keeping practice and what can be learned from it in focus:

> Holistic reflective practice represents the combination of technical reflection and practical and process reflection, which involved the practitioners focusing not only on what they did and how but also on why they or the clients acted or reacted in particular ways. (Ruch 2007, p.668)

Undertaking such holistic reflective practice must not be seen as just a challenge for individual family support practitioners but also for the managers supervising them and the learning culture of organisations as a whole. In drawing together a policy handbook, *The Agenda for Children's Services* (OMCYA 2007), as a focus for the delivery of a raft of policies promoting family support, the Irish government accepted that this could only be achieved through reflective practice at all levels of delivery. Accordingly, the handbook termed itself 'an active policy tool' and provided not only policy summaries, key concepts and explanatory frameworks, but also three sets of reflective questions addressed to staff involved in service delivery, to those in management and to those in policy-making. These questions all addressed a single set of service characteristics associated with family support, but did so phrased in a way that reflected the different concerns of the three types of staff. The materials were designed for ease of photocopying and scanning, and for the creation of interactive media to facilitate their use for reflective practice at all organisational levels by individuals, professional groups and operational teams, and at seminars, conferences, service reviews and case discussions. In this systemic fashion, reflective practice has a major role to play in promoting family support:

> It simultaneously emphasizes the need to understand the nature of complexity, uncertainty and risk in practice, and the necessary responses to these characteristics of social problems, alongside the importance of technical–rational knowledge and bureaucratic systems for effective interventions. (Ruch 2007, p.660)

THEORIES TO FRAME AND INFORM FAMILY SUPPORT

In order to engage in reflective practice in the field of family support, it is important to have a theoretical lens. As yet there is no distinct family support theory. There is, however, a wide range of relevant theory (Frost and Dolan 2012). In one way this is an inductive strength as it encourages theoretical flexibility through pursuit of theory that seems likely to be most helpful in describing and analysing particular family support experiences. However, such eclecticism begs the question of how theories get to be candidates for selection, and plays down the deductive aspect of reflective practice. There needs to be a theoretical underpinning to any family support work and an external theoretical framing to enable critical reflection. While family support is not a distinct theory in its own right, the position being advocated in this book is that there are four core constructs, each with an associated theoretical base, that usefully complement each other in a manner that provides a necessary theoretical foundation. The four constructs are social ecology, resilience, social support and social capital (Canavan *et al.* 2000). (See Figure 1.1.)

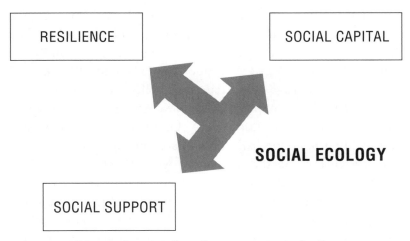

Figure 1.1: Theoretical sources for reflective practice in family support

Social ecology

Social ecology directs attention to 'the ways in which people and their habitats shape and influence one another through a process of reciprocal interactions between individuals and groups and their immediate and wider environments' (Jack 1997, p.109). In this way, it provides a contextualising theoretical orientation to thinking about family support. It emphasises the multiple dimensions to be considered in understanding the psychosocial development of children and young people – physical, social, economic and cultural environments as well as personal attributes. It also considers the multiple levels at which processes of development play out – within the individual, the immediate family, informal groups and formal organisations. Perhaps most importantly it has at its core a concern to give cognisance to the complexity of the cumulative impact of processes and events over time, expressed in both biographical and historical scale. 'Development is defined as the person's evolving conception of the ecological environment, and his relation to it, as well as the person's growing capacity to discover, sustain or alter its properties' (Bronfenbrenner 1979, p.9).

This approach is most clearly set out in the influential work of Urie Bronfenbrenner, with its powerful image of the developing child nested in four interlocking, interdependent systems. The first of these, the micro-system, is where the developing child experiences close relationships, positive and negative, with significant others such as parents and siblings, extended family and individuals from the neighbourhood and at school. Where these micro-systems engage or overlap, they collectively constitute the meso-system. For example, a child's meso-system might comprise the child's immediate family, the school that they attend and the neighbourhood football club they are a member of. Beyond the meso-system there lies the exosystem in which the child has no direct involvement but is affected by the influence it has over the first two systems. A parent's workplace and local political institutions may be key constituents of the exo-system. The fourth and overarching system is the macro-system. Here the spheres of law, economy and politics establish the ideological and organisational master pattern of the whole social formation in which the child's development takes place.

Resilience

At the core of resilience as an organising concept is the recognition that children and young people can achieve good outcomes in the face of significant adverse conditions through the interplay of risk and protective factors, internal and external to the child or young person. While there is no one agreed definition of resilience, whatever the emphasis in the definition of resilience, 'either implicit or explicit in all of them are concerns with development, adaptation and outcomes, coping with threats and adversity, individual and environment interaction, and supportive and undermining factors' (Canavan 2008, p.2).

To move right away from any lingering association of resilience with character traits and to make it applicable across cultures, one definition usefully emphasises that it refers not to the individual, but to a process of navigation and negotiation:

Definition: In the context of exposure to significant adversity, whether psychological, environmental, or both, resilience is both the capacity of individuals to navigate their way to health-sustaining resources, including opportunities to experience feelings of well-being, and a condition of the individual's family, community and culture to provide these health resources and experiences in culturally meaningful ways. (Ungar 2008, p.225)

Situated and de-centred in this way, resilience becomes more a characteristic of the social ecology of which the individual child or young person is a part rather than just of the individual. That said, even with this definition it remains the case that resilience can only be measured in terms of outcomes achieved by individuals relative to what was expected.

Resilience in young people from disadvantaged families has been found to be associated with a range of factors amenable to intervention and change: a secure attachment with a family member or other caregiver; having positive relationships with friends; a positive experience of some aspect of school; feeling in control over decisions in life; or being given the chance of a 'turning point', such as a new opportunity or a break from a high-risk area. A child may have experienced adversity in their early life, but there is still the opportunity of introducing into their lives at a later stage protective factors, such as providing supportive adult relationships and rewarding talents and interests. This can help build their resilience and counter previous disadvantage (Gilligan 2009a, b). Indeed, there is even evidence of 'steeling' effects in which successful coping with stress or adversity can lead to improved functioning and increased resistance to stress/adversity (Rutter 2012, pp.33–42).

Social support

Social support is the perception and the actuality of having assistance available from other people. In the main this support is accessed from the 'central helping system' (Dolan and Canavan 2000) of the informal networks of the nuclear and extended family, and to a lesser extent friends (Canavan and Dolan 2003, pp.179–192; Cutrona 2000). It is generally only when that support is perceived or experienced as weak, non-existent or incapable of offering the type or extent of help required that a person needing help will turn, or be directed, to formal sources of support. This is not to counterpose the informal and the formal as an 'either/or' choice. Informal support may appeal as generally offered at no cost, as non-stigmatising, and available outside of office hours, but there are types and degrees of need where professional help is clearly required (Gardner 2003). Thus formal support can both supplement and complement the informal. In addition, it is recognised that families can be the main source of stress and indeed abuse in children and young people's lives.

There are specific kinds and qualities of support available to families, with four main types identified (Cutrona 2000): concrete support, which relates to practical acts of assistance between people; emotional support, which comprises acts of empathy, listening and generally 'being there' for someone when needed; advice support, which goes beyond the advice itself to the reassurance that goes with it; and esteem support, which centres on how one person rates and informs another of their personal worth. It is also important to recognise that there are variations in the quality of support, and this is expressed in three major ways. First, closeness expresses the extent to which support can be assumed and given because of mutual affection between partners, near family members and long-established friends. A second dimension is reciprocity that involves activity whereby help is exchanged equally between people, and ensures that a person does not feel beholden to another – there is a comfort and security that goes with knowing that the exchange of support is available if and when it is needed. The third dimension is durability, which relates to the contact rates and length of time people are known to each other. Ideally reliable members are those who are known for a long period, are nearby to offer help, and typically are in no way intrusive.

Thus, social support theory draws on a considerable body of research to clearly identify the types and qualities of relationships that provide support in a way that can be concisely demonstrated and easily understood. As such, it can be directly applied in the field of family support including work with young people. From a social support perspective, the ultimate goal of family support is to achieve the rights of young people through meeting their needs within the family, and this, following the direction of social ecological theory, is dependent on ensuring a nested set of social supports. Children and young people require the support of immediate family. Family rests on the support of extended family, which in turn draws on a wider informal network of friends, neighbours and community. These various sources of informal support in turn need to be able to access a wide range of formal institutions within the statutory, community, voluntary and private sector to meet young people's educational, health and recreational needs, and give expression to their rights in these areas. It should also be recognised that the statutory, community, voluntary and private sectors require support from national policy and legislation.

From the nested model it is clear that social support is more than just the immediate network of nuclear and extended family relationships. It involves the entire social ecology in which they are located, including school and neighbourhood, community and statutory services, and national and international institutions. (See Figure 1.2.)

CHILD/YOUNG PERSON
Achieving rights and meeting needs

Immediate family

Extended family

Friends/neighbourhood

Formal organisations
(statutory, voluntary, community, commercial)

National social, economic, political, legal institutions

GLOBAL INSTITUTIONS AND PROCESSES

HISTORICAL AND BIOGRAPHICAL TIME

Figure 1.2: A cupped model of the social ecology of family support

Social capital

To acknowledge the range of resources within the nested model, it is helpful to introduce the concept of 'social capital' (Field 2003). Although still a contested and developing concept, social capital can helpfully be defined as 'the sum of the resources, actual or virtual, that accrue to an individual or a group by virtue of possessing a durable network of more or less institutionalised relationships of mutual acquaintance and recognition' (Bourdieu and Wacquant, cited in Henderson *et al.* 2007, p.12).

Three different types of social capital have been identified. *Bonding social capital* connects people with similar characteristics in relationships of solidarity based on shared experiences and values:

> Bonding capital is made up of the ties between people who are alike or who share a common experience, such as between family and friends. Bridging capital arises from the connections between groups of dissimilar people, such as different ethnic communities living in the same neighbourhood. Linking capital is used to mediate between different sectors and levels of society, for example between local government and community organisations. (Gilchrist, cited in Broadhead, Meleady and Delgado 2008, p.78)

Bridging social capital extends those relationships through connections a member of one network has with another. 'Bonding social capital constitutes a kind of sociological superglue, whereas bridging social capital provides a sociological WD-40' (Putnam, cited in Barry 2012, p.56).

There is also *linking social capital*, which is a relationship between an individual and figure of power outside of their informal networks, such as a government official or politician.

It is important to recognise that all forms of social capital are based on active contact:

> ...developed in our relationships, through doing things for one another and the trust that we develop in one another. It helps in bonding fragmented social life; in the bridging of communities to places and contacts beyond their immediate environment and

in the linking of people to formal structures and agencies that they may need for help with opportunities for education and employment. (Catts and Ozga, cited in Allan and Catts 2012, p.6)

It is also important to note that there can be negative features to social capital. It can exclude as well as include and reinforce oppressive hierarchies of power within social networks based, for example, on age, gender and class. However, *the development, or 'banking', of social capital* as personal assets has been highlighted as a possible part of the solution to helping people access positive and durable support in their lives as and when they need it. In that sense, family support interventions can be seen as a form of social capital building (Jack and Jordan 1999). Thus social capital can be viewed as 'developmental assets' realised through effective social support. For some families, realising this personal potential will require additional formal family support interventions aimed at bolstering the type and quality of social support available to them.

It is clear that these four theories are connected and share common elements – for example, the link between social support enlistment and utilisation of bonding and bridging social capital and resilience building is established (Dolan 2008; Ungar 2012). They also do not exhaust all the possible theoretical perspectives that may be helpful in developing reflective practice in family support, and indeed may suggest other areas. For example, citizenship and civic engagement link well and have strong theoretical resonance. The literature on youth civic engagement suggests that when young people become active citizens with opportunities to volunteer, specific benefits accrue – mastery, belonging and generosity development. These benefits can accrue for all young people, including those in adversity and in need of most support (Shaw *et al.* 2014). Thus, through their civic engagement, young people and parents can create new network sources for additional social support and the potential to enable better wellbeing and/or well-becoming (Dolan 2012). Second, by being civically active there is respite for a person from their own difficulties and new knowledge that they are not the only person experiencing difficulty. This can assist the person in coping and in their attainment of better perceived resiliency. Third, in relation to social capital and ecological contexts, citizenship can bring personal and collective positive opportunities that may otherwise lie unknown or dormant for an individual family and/or community (Redmond and Dolan 2012).

A DEFINITION OF FAMILY SUPPORT

The set of core concepts set out in the previous section, based on the experience captured in the growing literature and garnered from active engagement in the field, provides family support with its theoretical foundations. But for its further development, both theoretically and in practice, family support needs a definition. We previously developed the following definition:

> Family support is both a style of work and a set of activities that reinforce positive informal social networks through integrated programmes. These programmes combine statutory, voluntary, community and private services and are generally provided to families within their own homes and communities. The primary focus of these services is on early intervention, aiming to promote and protect the health, wellbeing and rights of all children, young people and their families. At the same time, particular attention is given to those who are vulnerable or at risk. (Dolan *et al.* 2006, p.16)

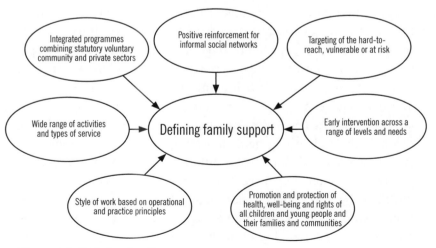

Figure 1.3: Defining family support
Source: Dolan et al. (2006, p.16)

Components of family support

By combining the elements covered by the definition in a single statement, an important point is being made about the integrated nature of family support. Based on the definition, it is possible to identify seven components that need to be present in any family support policy and service design. The particular form the components take will be dependent on the specific circumstance, but they need to be clearly identifiable, and must either deliver or actively allow for:

- promotion of both rights and outcomes

- meshing with informal social support

- cross-sectoral integration

- early intervention

- breadth of provision

- outreach to socially excluded groups

- reflective style of work based on family support practice principles.

Each component should have equal attention and each needs to be present. While it is helpful to identify the core components of family support in a definition, it is vital not to deny the complexity and contested aspects of the purpose, process and outcomes associated with it. They, too, must be part of the description and analysis required for reflective practice.

Family support as a style of practice

The definition makes it clear that family support is not just the description of a set of services and design features; it is also a style of practice. Again, directed by the definition, ten principles of family support practice are as follows:

- Child-centred: family support requires a clear focus on the wishes, feelings, safety and wellbeing of children.

- Needs-led: family support interventions are needs-led and strive for the minimum intervention required.

- Strengths-based: family support services reflect a strengths-based perspective that is mindful of resilience as a characteristic of many children and families' lives.

- Socially inclusive: services aim to promote social inclusion, addressing issues around ethnicity, disability and rural/urban communities.

- Partnership-based: working in partnership is an integral part of family support. Partnership includes children, families, professionals and communities.

- Informal network-focused: family support promotes the view that effective interventions are those that strengthen informal support networks.

- Easily accessed: families are encouraged to self-refer, and multi-access referral paths will be facilitated.

- Responsive and flexible: family support is responsive and flexible in respect of location, timing, setting and changing needs, and can incorporate both child protection and out of home care.

- Collaborative in development: involvement of service users and providers in the planning, delivery and evaluation of family support services is promoted on an ongoing basis.

- Evidence-informed: measures of success are routinely built into provision so as to facilitate evaluation based on attention to the outcomes for service users, and thereby to facilitate ongoing support for quality services based on best practice.

This set of definitional material, particularly the principles, is revisited throughout the remaining chapters of the book.

FRAMEWORK AND LAYOUT OF THE REMAINDER OF THIS BOOK

From the foundations laid in this introduction, an explicit position is further built up through four subsequent chapters focusing in turn on 'Policy and politics', 'Management and leadership', 'Direct practice' and 'Monitoring and evaluation', before concluding the book with a call to action for 'Globalising family support'. In Chapter Two, on policy and politics, we focus on family support as an issue for the national policy level, the second-to-last level of the cupped model (see Figure 1.2). Although distant in social space from the nitty-gritty of formal and informal provision of family support, we argue that full understanding of its provenance, shape and value at the individual level requires engagement with the political and policy level. Thus, the central argument of this chapter is that family support is necessarily a political project, grounded in assumptions about the nature of family and the respective roles of state and civil society in its provision. The degree to which family support will be promoted or impeded will depend on the dominant discourse in society on these matters. Drawing on classic work on the international comparative analysis of welfare states, we consider how family support can be characterised in different welfare state regimes, before connecting this analysis with Hardiker *et al.*'s approach to understanding need and service provision within a narrower child welfare frame. From the emerging synthesis is a set of policy possibilities for family support. The UK's experience of the New Labour government is used as a case example through which these policy possibilities are explored.

Working forward from the policy level, Chapter Three addresses management and leadership in family support. The task in this chapter is not to set out a series of detailed prescriptions across all aspects of what is traditionally understood as service management and leadership – we take it as given that these can be accessed in other places. Rather, we consider the value of a small number of current ideas emerging from management and related fields. Unsurprisingly, Chapter Three starts with a focus on planning – here, we argue in favour of the adoption of theory of change approaches within planning for family support, and within this the use of logic modelling as a technical approach in their development. We support these approaches because they allow theories to be made explicit and testable, although we also identify the complexity and risks involved. One key question for any plan is, what is the ideal organisational infrastructure required to support its implementation? Chapter Three explores two related governance ideas – post-modern organisations and boundary-spanning leaders – as resonating strongly with family support. Reflective of whole child, ecological orientations, these approaches recognise the need for family support organisations, leaders and staff to be outward-looking, flexible and non-bureaucratic, and directed towards working with other agencies and professionals. Also examined is the potential for family support governance to create meaningful opportunities for participation by children and parents. But alongside these externally directed activities, we recognise that effective family support management requires a sharp internal focus on supporting and supervising staff, in their work directly with children, young people and parents, and with other organisations. Towards this we identify key dimensions of staff support and offer a set of empirically based principles for family support management. We also explore the potential of reflective practice, particularly within supervision, as key to supporting staff and ensuring their wellbeing.

Family support is only truly meaningful when it is embodied in practice. Chapter Four provides a framework for mapping practice and some key guidance on how to do it. The chapter's start-point is a brief description of the landscape of family support practice. Within this, the dimensions of needs, stage of development, setting and provision as targeted or universal, as well as the focus of intervention as developmental, protective or compensatory, are discussed. Also explored in this mapping exercise is a key question for modern family support – what should be the balance between programmatic approaches and individually delivered practice that develops organically in a relationship-based context? Two brief case studies follow that exemplify these practice dimensions. The next part of the chapter demonstrates how each of family support's framing theories has concrete application in practice. The final part offers reflective practice as a compass for a worker in quality assuring and enhancing their work, within this emphasising empathy as central to good relationship-based working, before proposing the family support principles as a tool for practice and reflection. Through the chapter, key prompts for good practice are presented.

That family support practice will make a difference to those receiving it is a fundamental assumption of this book, but this needs to be established on a continuing basis. The importance of evaluation to family support is signified in its inclusion as one of the ten principles. In Chapter Five, we develop the argument that the nature of family support requires a bespoke form of evaluation. We build the case for family support evaluation by first illustrating the current context for the operation of programme evaluation, wherein the demand exists for policy to be based on evidence and where services are under constant scrutiny to demonstrate their value. We stress the need for evaluation to be theoretically driven: by core and emerging theories for family support; by theories of change; by theories of implementation; and by reflective practice theories. In an era dominated by attention to outcomes, we emphasise the importance of understanding family support processes (using the family support principles as a guide) and practice.

Critically, following Schwandt (2005), and echoing the key message from Chapter Three, we argue for an approach to the evaluation of practice that doesn't start from a view that it needs to change. We recognise the importance of outcomes, but tease out and elaborate a more layered approach to understanding and measuring them. In this regard we make a particular argument for seeking depth and developing 'thick' outcomes. Together these various imperatives suggest the need for a mixed-methods strategy for family support evaluation. The imperatives also accord well with a wider epistemological commitment to realist evaluation as proposed by Pawson (2006), wherein evaluation should seek to establish what works, for whom, and in what circumstances. Based on this underpinning realist epistemology, family support evaluation must be sensitive to service contexts that are affected by multiple factors and aimed at uncovering the often hidden mechanisms that help explain why services work or not.

Introducing the global to the cupped model for family support recognises this ecological level source of influence all the way into the day-to-day lives of children, informing and sometimes transforming the levels of the nation-state family support ecology on the way. Adding this level to our model also recognises that there is a promise in family support, that it can be meaningful and helpful to children and families, beyond the Global North where much of the current thinking has been done. Our final chapter addresses these issues. Chapter Six outlines a general argument for the value of comparative approaches to social policy analysis before exploring the meaning of globalisation and some dilemmas and tensions of global family support. It then follows Payne (2006) in developing an analytical framework for the internationalisation of family support. UNICEF's programme on social protection and family support, 'Family and parenting support: policies, practice and outcomes', is suggested as the basis on which a concrete programme of international research and action on family support could proceed. The chapter concludes by restating key messages from this book as the conceptual foundation on which such a programme could be built.

— *Chapter Two* —

THE POLICY AND POLITICS OF FAMILY SUPPORT

INTRODUCTION

In Chapter One a cupped model was presented as a way of representing the social ecology of family support (see Figure 1.2). As part of advocating for a clear position on family support as an overarching paradigm for child welfare, it was argued that the rights, needs and responsibilities of both children and their parents should be seen to be dependent on formal and informal resources at a range of levels. This can be illustrated by thinking about a young person developing their adolescent identity who is an enthusiastic football player, gaining self-respect and honing physical and social skills through the sport. The young person benefits from the encouragement of parents, wider family and friends. Playing football is part of the activities of a neighbourhood youth club run by volunteers with the financial support of a local shopkeeper. Matches are played on council pitches upgraded through central government-targeted funding, made available in line with a national sports strategy committed to by the government as part of a national report to the UN Committee on the Rights of the Child.

This chapter aims to draw attention to the lower levels of the cupped model. It focuses on the national level – in Bronfenbrenner's (1979) terms, the macro-systems of cultural, economic and political institutions and processes. These need to be understood and addressed as generating a policy dynamic that promotes or impedes the development of family support throughout all levels of the social ecology. Managing that dynamic is a 'political project' in that power relationships within and between civil society, the state and the economy as 'sites of power' (Smith 2008) all need to be engaged with. This is not just a challenge to politicians and policy-makers but to anyone engaged in family support.

It is important to recognise that these power relationships play out across sites in a dispersed as well as focused fashion, with unintended as well as intended consequences. Returning to the illustration of the young footballer above, the government of one political colour may, through promoting a national sports strategy, have inadvertently won the shopkeeper (who has political ambitions as a member of a different political party) local support from voters who appreciate him sponsoring a club that ironically might not exist for him to sponsor without central government funds made available by his political opponents:

> As it [policy] moves from one place to another, from one site to another and from one level to another, it is revised, inflected, appropriated and bent in encounters of different kinds. A policy then is never a completed object. Indeed in the process of policy movement, sites and levels themselves may become unsettled, reformed and reconnected in new ways. This does not mean that each moment makes something new or different, but that the outcomes of these movements and moments cannot be wholly prescribed from its starting point. Indeed understood in this way, policy is always subject to revisions and inflections, which opens up a politics of translation in which there are always possibilities at stake. Policy, then, is necessarily unfinished. (Clarke *et al.* 2015, pp.15–16)

Promoting family support within this fluid but constrained context requires strategies of accommodation and compromise along with strategies of resistance and control. The aim of this chapter is to suggest how to analyse and engage with this politics of family support, including its 'disturbing logic' (Parker 1990, p.99), which tends to call into question the distribution of power and resources within socially and economically hierarchical societies. Consideration is given to how the understanding of family support proposed in Chapter One can help with both mobilising and managing change through promoting reflective practice in regard to policy. This mobilising and management of change constitutes the politics of family support.

While politics is more than just the activity of the state, it is important to start with a brief review of the imperative for the state to address the family as a social policy issue at all. The varied social policy perspectives on the family are noted, and then an approach proposed to advance family support, as defined in Chapter One. This perspective is based on an updating of the seminal work of Hardiker, Exton and Barker (1991) on prevention in children's services. Its use is illustrated by considering a key period of family support development in England under New Labour (1997–2010).

We picked this UK example because it contains a rich, often contradictory, mix of legislative, policy and service initiatives. These focus on 'the family' as the core institution of civil society as part of a much wider state modernisation strategy driven by neo-liberal economic concerns and the politics of social democracy in a period of globalisation (Jordan and Drakeford 2012). It is argued that family support should indeed be part of just some such ambitious strategic project, but not one that is driven from above. The ecological perspective and practice principles set out in Chapter One take the position that family support cannot be delivered from above, but must be part of a politics of a developmental, democratic dialogue between the state and civil society (Patel 2005). The chapter ends with a series of reflective questions providing a starting point for undertaking a political appraisal of national opportunities for advancing family support as a paradigm for child welfare as state policy.

SOCIAL POLICY AND THE FAMILY

That the family continues to be one of the core institutions of contemporary society across the globe is indisputable. What this actually means in lived experience, however, is quite a different matter:

One of the major distinctions between traditional and more recent approaches to the family is the shift away from the idea of 'the family' as a *social institution* governed by rigid moral conventions to an idea of family and wider personal life as diverse sets of *practices*. (Chambers 2012, p.33; emphasis in original)

One way to try and empirically capture the diverse forms of this universal social unit is to abandon the notion of family in favour of a term such as 'household': 'a social category which has been used as a common way of "fixing" people in particular places at particular times for the purposes of counting and categorising' (Ribbens McCarthy, Doolittle and Day Sclater 2008, p.93). In this way the physical boundaries of any particular form of housing being used by an identifiable social unit allows for categorisation and counting – for example, single-parent households with children under five in rented social housing can be distinguished from two-parent households with adolescent children in mortgaged private sector housing. But this tidy technical solution is at risk of missing the point – what is important about families, whatever form they take, is that they bring together the biological, economic, cultural and emotional dimensions to people's lives in a particularly potent fashion. The multiplicity and ambivalence of family experiences is what they are about, as nicely captured here:

> While it is true that many of our happiest moments and our closest relationships are within families it is also true that such fulfilment can be found with people and in settings outside our family. In reality as well as being the source of many positive experiences... there are also a whole range of negative experiences in families, ranging from plain unhappiness to abuse, neglect and exploitation. (Frost and Stein 1989, p.5)

It is therefore not surprising that family, as such a key institution of civil society, should be the object of interest to the state. The obligations it creates, particularly for women, in regard to dependent relationships based on age, young and old, sickness and disability, are deeply embedded in the normative structures of particular social formations. Family in its various forms carries with it assumptions about how cultural, social, spiritual and moral values should be instilled and sustained. Varied family practices support the social, emotional and material needs of its members in relatively predictable ways, ensuring nurture and the provision of socially necessary care. Even in social formations that thrive on possessive individualism, the collective wellbeing of the members of families is valorised and expected to provide security, belonging, connectedness and companionship. At the same time, sustaining these expectations and functions, 'doing' and 'displaying' family (Dermott and Seymour 2011; Ribbens McCarthy *et al.* 2008), is constantly being negotiated and re-negotiated between particular individuals as socially defined opportunities and expectations change and are contested. The extent and form of state interest and intervention in the family varies over time, both biographical and historical time, and according to place, culture, politics and economic systems (Chambers 2012; Wells 2009).

The challenge to engaging in the politics of the shifting and contested space of family policy requires that those involved first clarify from within the political perspectives and institutional arrangements of any particular nation-state what the expectations are of families, and what aspects and outcomes for families are regarded as needing state support.

FAMILY SUPPORT AS A POLICY CHOICE

To help tease out the state engagement with families that best expresses the complex, participatory and inclusive family support being advocated in this book, it is helpful to turn to the seminal ideas of Hardiker, Exton and Barker on preventative child welfare. Over 25 years ago, Hardiker and her colleagues (1991) developed a set of social policy models of prevention in children's services. Their work remains unequalled in its attention to the detail and logic of technical modelling linked to recognition that what is in question is as much about political vision as it is service design. It is important to acknowledge that Hardiker and her colleagues did not use 'family support' as a term for an overarching paradigm in the way that it is being done within this book. For them, family support was just a type of service found within one model of prevention. However, with some modification, their work on prevention has been shown to usefully extend into an explanatory framework for family support in the widest sense (Pinkerton, Higgins and Devine 2000).

The modelling by Hardiker and her colleagues provides a useful bridge between a number of alternative broad social policy perspectives that still have currency (Daly 2011), and the needs and services characteristic of different levels of family support. This is achieved by creating 'an imperfect but hopefully enlightening synthesis' (Hardiker *et al.* 1991, p.18) of two analytical frameworks – one dealing with types of welfare and the other with levels of provision. When combined into a third conceptual framework, a wide range of options as to what might constitute family support becomes apparent. Within these options three relatively consistent models of family support can be constructed as alternative policy positions. A first step in the development of a politics of family support is being clear on which of these models is being pursued.

But to return to Hardiker and her colleagues' starting point – they accept that in regard to welfare provision in general, and child welfare in particular, there are a number of directions a government may choose to go. They argue that there are three major alternatives based on differing assumptions about social need and how it should be met. These they term 'residual', 'institutional' and 'developmental'. The different perspectives are distinguished on the basis of how they each address both the 'construction of social problems' and the 'role of the state in the provision of welfare' (see Table 2.1) – in other words, what needs are regarded as important and what service responses by the state are appropriate.

Table 2.1: Linking types of welfare to social problems and state provision

Types of welfare	Construction of social problems (needs)	Role of the state in providing welfare (services)
Residual	Individualised explanations Personal pathology Individual deficit	Individual/family carries burden of responsibility to provide for all needs Individual/family has the right/responsibility to choose services State provides basic social minimum as a last resort/ safety net Informal, voluntary and private sources of care are predominant
Institutional	Product of faulty interaction between individual and environment Faulty functioning of either individual or social institutions Individual needs help to adjust to demands of society Improvements may be needed in delivery of welfare services	State has a duty to ensure needs of most disadvantaged members of society are met State discharges its duty by coordinating mixed economy of welfare in which other agencies, such as faith-based organisations, play a significant role
Developmental	Individual difficulties arise from the unequal distribution of power and resources in society Individuals need to be able to exert more control over their lives including increased access to resources Social systems, not people, are required to change	State guarantees social rights State accepts predominant responsibility for meeting social needs via universal social services and redistributive social policies State welfare is a means towards a just and equal society

Source: Modified from Hardiker et al. (1991)

To greatly simplify, governments taking a residual position with regard to need as about individual shortcomings accept as fit cause for state intervention only the most extreme situations that fall beyond the means of civil society, and in particular, beyond the social support capacity of families. Even then, in order not to be seen as offering better support than the informal systems, intervention has to be minimalist. Governments committed to an institutional position see need as primarily resulting from a dysfunction in relations between individuals and society that require state intervention to correct or to manage, generally in conjunction with other institutions, such as faith-based organisations or charities. The developmental position regards need as reflecting the unequal nature of existing society and the inevitable overburdening of many informal support networks, of which the family is one. Accordingly, the state needs to take a major lead responsibility in meeting need through putting in place formal support systems providing universal, redistributive services.

Hardiker and her colleagues' framework linking type of welfare to how social problems are regarded and what view is taken to state provision can be used to characterise particular welfare administrative systems, policies and practices. It provides a means of understanding the type of family support generally available at a particular point in a country's history. This allows for the second step in developing a politics of family support – judgement on whether what exists is in accordance with or contrary to the type of family support aspired to. Pursuit of developmental family support in a country where the residual approach is being taken requires a politics of opposition and alternative, whereas, if an institutional approach is being taken, a politics of development and reconfiguring is required. In other words, in the first case, trying to establish a network of community-based family centres in a country where a right-wing government is ideologically opposed to public spending requires a strategy based on community action creating a network of low-budget family centres alongside active support for opposition political parties and movements. By contrast, in the second scenario, where a government is prepared to back some state services and fund non-governmental organisation

(NGO) provision, the strategy would be to network across all types of family centres promoting developmental family support, developing demonstration projects and lobbying for government policy and funding support.

The framework can also be used to examine the coherence or otherwise of the relationship between a particular system and the policies and practices within it (Pinkerton *et al.* 2000). Not only does this allow different policy options to be clarified, but it can also reveal shifts that may be occurring within a system, whether intentionally or by default. Identifying such systemic shifts and contradictions is central to the political appraisal of the potential for family support. They represent the basis on which a strategy for mobilising and managing the shift towards a desired approach to a family support paradigm can be analysed and turned into an action plan. So, in the illustration above, a lukewarm government response to the strategy of development and reconfiguration, that is, demonstration projects and lobbying, might be revealing that government policy has shifted towards a more residualist view, but without that being made explicit.

The second framework Hardiker and her colleagues use for their model-building directly addresses child welfare (see Table 2.2). It describes different levels of prevention, and draws on a generally accepted adaptation for children's services of a standard three-part classification from preventative medicine (Frost and Dolan 2012; Frost *et al.* 2015; Parker 1990). Level 1 comprises universally available services that can be expected to strengthen family functioning. Level 2 is made up of support services targeted at families in early difficulties, where the risks of breakdown remain low. Level 3 involves work with families who are suffering severe and established difficulties. Hardiker and her colleagues added a Level 4 to cover children and young people in out-of-home care and their need to leave care in a way that minimises the ill effects resulting from either their separation from family, including its causes, or their involvement with the care system. The aim of intervention at this level is to minimise the length of time they spend in substitute care, and to facilitate their reintegration into social care networks outside of the formal care system. Each level represents a deeper degree of state intervention into family life. How this deeper penetration of the state into family life is viewed varies according to whether a 'residual', 'institutional' or 'developmental' perspective is being pursued.

Table 2.2: Models of family support

Levels of involvement	Types of welfare		
	Residual	Institutional	Developmental
Level 1			Primary developmental model
Level 2		Secondary institutional model	
Level 3	Tertiary residual model		
Level 4			

Source: Modified from Hardiker et al. (1991)

Through combining the 'welfare types' and 'levels of prevention' frameworks, Hardiker and her colleagues created a third framework that can be recast as models of family support (Pinkerton *et al.* 2000). As can be seen in Table 2.2, this allows for specific services to be located in any one of 12 possible positions, expressing level of intervention and type of welfare. Each of these has its own implications for identifying need and also for delivering services. More importantly for the argument here, the three most coherent couplings of 'level of prevention' and 'type of welfare' can be combined to produce three models – 'primary developmental', 'secondary institutional' and 'tertiary residual'. Services with particular characteristics are likely to be associated with each model (see Table 2.3).

Table 2.3: Models of family support with characteristic services

Model of family support	Associated services
Primary developmental	Proactive provision in response to locally identified issues
	Accessible, localised services
	Resources to strengthen and develop existing helping networks
	Provision of day care facilities for children
	Advice, information and advocacy services
	Decentralised management structures involving service users
Secondary institutional	Advice and information services
	Early detection and rapid response duty and intake systems
	Focused and time-limited social work interventions
	Parenting support services
	Social care planning to mobilise packages of care
	Practical and material support linked to social work intervention
Tertiary residual	Interventions targeted on situations of imminent admission to care
	Rigorous gate keeping around entry into care systems
	Concentration on statutory social work
	Narrowly defined casework interventions
	Short-term, rapid closure interventions

The configuration of a national child welfare system to ensure one or other type of family support will require attention to the levels of intervention being targeted and to the type of welfare being promoted. So, for example, the view of a complex, participatory and inclusive family support being advocated by this book is certainly not compatible with a tertiary residual model, and it is arguable whether it can be achieved by the secondary institutional model. Where it sits most comfortably is within the primary developmental model. That said, it needs to be stressed that there will never only be one level of intervention. The three models can be regarded as contending positions on family support based on where the focus of policy development and resource allocation should be.

The struggle around which of these models is being pursued constitutes the core of the politics of family support. Choices between the three positions on family support tend to be taken in the arena of formal politics, with parties on the right of the political spectrum supporting the tertiary residual model and those on the left taking a primary developmental position. But it is important not to restrict the politics of family support to formal politics. To help with this, it is useful to recognise that much of what makes it into government policy and indeed law will have come out of the activity of a 'policy community', and this, in turn, will draw on information, encouragement, criticism and inspiration from an 'issue network' (Bochel and Bochel 2004; Pinkerton 2006).

A policy community is characterised by a limited number of participants in the policy process, constant in their presence and consistent in their values and policy preferences, all with resources behind their involvement, having frequent and high-quality interaction and sharing a significant degree of consensus about the policy process as well as their broad policy preferences. They are the 'stakeholders' that the government is likely to directly engage with and often encourage. By contrast, an 'issue network' is made up of many more numbers and types of actors whose interests in the issue can be very diverse, whose involvement will fluctuate, and among whom relationships, where they exist, will vary from collaboration to hostility. This much looser but more inclusive set of actors represents the reality that there are many more avenues to participation in the policy process than being elected politicians, state functionaries or professional employees in stakeholder organisations. Pressure on policy can be exerted by membership of political parties and pressure groups, voting in elections and referenda, giving user feedback on public services, 'direct action' protest and lifestyle choices.

Through thinking about family support as linked to wider social policy assumptions about types of welfare with different levels of intervention, with the associated sets of needs and services, and with specific types of childcare services, it becomes clear that there is no one, exclusive, correct approach to family support. Rather, what form it takes will involve political choices about developing a policy position with a view to prioritising a particular level of intervention in accordance with wider political concerns. These wider political concerns and policy positions need to be made explicit, along with what implications they have for family support. As noted earlier, these are tendencies, not exclusive positions, but do require one to be dominant if there is to be policy coherence. The policy dynamic within any child welfare system is generated by the shifting balance between the emphases being given to each. The skill of policy analysis is to reveal within a child welfare system at any particular point in its history shifts that may be occurring within it, whether intentionally or by default. As will be illustrated in the next section, identifying such systemic shifts and contradictions is central to the political appraisal of the potential for family support at any point in time.

FAMILY SUPPORT UNDER NEW LABOUR

After 18 years of Conservative government, which, under Margaret Thatcher's leadership, saw the unbridled embrace of neo-liberalism, the Labour Party returned to office in 1997 with a landslide victory and the prefix 'New'. The political philosophy of New Labour, influenced by sociological 'Third Way' theory, was presented as a renewal of social democracy (Giddens 1998; Jordan 2000). New Labour was committed to the traditional goal of social democratic politics to manage capitalism in order to advance socialism, but believed that the impact of globalisation had fundamentally altered the political playing field. These changed circumstances required a focus on social justice rather than equality, and the use of free markets nationally and internationally, to deliver economic efficiency and growth through opening up new opportunities for individual achievement. These opportunities were exemplified in the ease of access to information worldwide provided by new information technologies, and ever more porous social boundaries open to all sorts of economic, cultural and political influences (B. Axford 2013; Sassen 2007; Smith 2008; Yeates 2001).

Entranced by the apparent pace and direction of change driven by globalisation, along with the size of their electoral victory, New Labour pursued a radical 'modernisation' project aimed at repositioning and boosting the UK in the global market. This included the review and overhaul of state welfare provision. Under the auspices of modernisation it actively set out to construct an inherently unstable hybrid of primary developmental and tertiary residual models discussed in the previous section:

> Much of its ambivalence, and many of the apparent contradictions that seem to characterise its [New Labour's] strategies and policies, is derived from the fact that, perhaps for the first time since the mid-19th century, the government is one that is constructing a futuristic project, precarious in its nature and profoundly ambitious in design. (Hendrick 2003, p.234)

In regard to child welfare, the challenge for New Labour was to review why the Children Act 1989 and its underpinning government-commissioned research had failed to refocus provision away from reacting to child abuse to promoting prevention. Family support services to 'children in need', as mandated by Part III of the Act, had not become the defining characteristic of child welfare. In the terms that New Labour had set itself, this could not be the well- established social democratic commitment to shift the axis of the system from Level 3 and 4 interventions, which their Conservative predecessors had been prepared to settle for, to Level 1 – a political choice between the tertiary residual and the primary developmental (see Table 2.2). Their hybrid model required something different. A high-level policy review led to the problem being defined, not as the need for relocation of resource to support rather than police families, but rather how to ensure opportunities for children and families under stress to take them out of social exclusion. Pathways into, and therefore out of, poverty were seen as a function of risk and protective factors. Families were identified as central to determining the balance of these risk and protective factors creating social inclusion or exclusion. In the main, families, with state investment, were the means to produce and sustain socially and economically useful citizens (Featherstone 2006; Gillies 2005).

If the Children Act mandate for delivering services to children in need had extended the canvas for state intervention in family life, New Labour's 'Every Child Matters' policy took it even wider:

> The vision we have is a shared one. Every child having an opportunity to fulfil their potential. And no child slipping through the net. (DfES 2004, cited in Morris 2012, p.15)

For the majority of families this was a social contract with the government that New Labour assumed they were ready and willing to take up. While a committed policy community had been constructed around a relatively coherent policy position, this had been done on the basis of a centrally driven technocratic perspective, with multiple sector delivery systems for disseminating policy developments. In terms of an issue network, this was not recognised as the necessary seed bed for effective policy shifts. There was no attempt to engage nor to dialogue with a wider range of potential interested parties. In so far as a wider debate was engaged in, it involved managing the media and electoral appeal rather than anything coming close to engaging and mobilising a broad-based constituency for change.

From within the technocratic frame of New Labour, family was, in the main, seen as a protective factor, but one requiring investment. In particular, some families were seen as requiring targeted support from integrated services to shift them from being on the risk side of the equation to the protective side. In order to combine the primary developmental with the tertiary residual, the financial cost of that support was framed as an economic investment (Fawcett *et al.*, cited in Morris 2012), thereby switching the problem from one of political choices about the redistribution of resources through state intervention, to a technical one of how to ensure optimum return on expenditure. Often cited in support of the position was how the Nobel prize-winning economist James Heckman had demonstrated that to invest in early years services led to the development of cognitive and social skills in young children. It was said that the US Perry Preschool programme yielded more than US$8 for every

US$1 invested through educational attainment, making for more capable and productive adults contributing to the economy rather than depending on public services and state benefits.

Interagency working became a central theme within policy, with the legal mandate and policy guidance from the Children Act 2004 moving policy away from local authority support to children in need towards a raft of locality-based but central government-driven programmes such as Sure Start, the Children Fund and Connexions, aimed at responding to the perceived risks of social exclusion. The aim was to promote social inclusion – overcoming barriers and reducing inequalities between the least advantaged groups and communities and the rest of society by recognising the potential of those who were marginalised, and opening up opportunities for that potential to be realised. The technical framing of this centralised policy encouraged efforts to monitor and research its outcomes. The results showed disappointingly slow returns on investment, and the families with the highest levels of need and more complex and enduring difficulties were not being engaged. This resulted in a shift in focus to those high-risk groups being seen as high-cost through their unwillingness and/or inability to play their role in partnership with government.

What followed was narrowly targeted policy, such as Respect and Think Family, aimed at the 4 per cent of families who, it was calculated, presented with multiple and complex needs. These were families where children were at risk of entering the care and protection systems, who experienced drug and alcohol problems, lived with violence and poverty, and required extensive state expenditure. These were the families of 'children in need' who were now 'at-risk' families. The attempt to hybridise the primary developmental and tertiary residual model had given way to the latter coming to the fore, with children of families at risk becoming the focus:

> Family support as a conceptual framework in child and family policy making has therefore changed. It is no longer a localised process to assess children and provide their families with services

based on thresholds of need. Instead, families are a site for intervention and partnership, whether cooperatively or coercively. Families are seen as central to the future production of responsible and productive citizens, and family support is now within a very different agenda. (Morris 2012, p.18)

Following the financial crisis of 2008 and the victory of a Conservative-led coalition in 2010, that 'very different agenda' was sharpened with reduced provision and more directly targeted services. Sure Start, for example, was to be taken 'back to its original purpose of early intervention, increase its focus on the neediest of families and better involve organisations with a track record of supporting families' (HM Government, cited in Frost *et al.* 2015, p.19). A new policy community was gathered around a residualist government preoccupied with its fiscal strategy, rolling back state intervention and protecting the economic status quo. That transition to a tertiary residual family support was made easy by the absence of any attempt by New Labour to engage with an issue network and establish a broad constituency for change. It had failed to provide an environment in which an alternative policy community and the shift towards a primary development family support could be sustained as part of an authentically new politics – a democratic dialogue between the developmental state and civil society.

PRIMARY DEVELOPMENTAL POLICY AGENDA

As the experience of New Labour demonstrated, unless family support policy is securely anchored in a developmental welfare approach and a set of institutions that has a core policy community, influencing and being influenced by an issue network and mobilising a wider constituency for change, it loses direction. To avoid this loss of direction, political advocates and policy-makers should aim to ensure that whatever the specific focus and design of a service, it will incorporate most, if not all, of the summarised components in Chapter One. Services will need to:

- share the central goal of promoting and protecting the health, wellbeing and rights of all children and young people, their families and their communities

- combine in an integrated fashion statutory, voluntary/community and private sectors

- positively reinforce informal social support networks

- reach out to marginalised, vulnerable, at-risk populations

- provide a wide range of activities and types of services

- offer access to early intervention across a range of levels

- reflect a style of work based on the ten practice principles.

Such family support requires strong coherent and consistent central government policy focused on ensuring organisational support and practice methods that work together to promote a primary developmental model of family support. Just as the family enhances the capacity of its members to grow and develop through resourcing the full range of individual needs (emotional, intellectual, social, cultural and material), so, too, family support policy has to address how best to promote a wide range of developmental needs. While securely focused on the primary developmental level of needs and services, policy must also encompass the other levels of need and matched services (see Table 2.3). Families with more complex needs require more complex services, for which the state must take lead responsibility.

Level 1 provides open access support to families (such as a public health nurse or GP services) and health promotion and information services (such as advice on good parenting). Level 2 support (such as pre-school provision), while still provided to families at their request, is targeted by assessment of need and mandated by the state as part of its responsibility towards supporting family life. At Level 3, support (such as social work home visiting) is better described as an intervention to indicate that the voluntary element is gone because severe and established difficulties placing children at risk have been assessed, and work with the family is mandated by law, often through the courts. At Level 4, the need within a family is so acute or the coping capacity so weak that children and young people have to be placed in medium or long-term out-of-home care. Work at Level 4 is also about lowering the level of need and/or improving coping so that re-engagement with services at the lower levels can become sufficient. The closer services are to providing for the self-assessed needs of families and children, the more likely they are to be accessed.

Family support needs to be primarily focused at Level 1, and be provided on an open access basis as part of community development. Not every family will require or want to use these services, but they should have access to them. Again, as in families themselves, family support policy must be about protection from harm as well as for promoting their wellbeing and development (e.g., education, play/leisure, built environment, child protection). Services must also be able to meet different levels of need and have a special responsibility where the level of need is greatest (e.g., acute illness, disability, school refusal, law breaking, homelessness, rural isolation, ethnic/cultural difference, poverty). Every effort should be made to provide easy access to services through outreach to individual children, their families and their communities. This requires making available non-stigmatising, multiple access points. Services also need to make full use of collaborative cross-referrals.

Policy needs to be concerned with ensuring vertical integration of provision through facilitating movement between levels and accessing services from across levels. The goal for a young mother leaving care (Level 4) should be to move down through the levels to a point where she only requires access to universal services on demand at Level 1. While still at Level 4 she should be able to access a community nurse (Level 1), be assessed for a pre-school service (Level 2) as well as join a support group for young mothers on the edge of care (Level 3). This vertical integration needs to be matched by attention to horizontal integration. Families will often benefit from a range of services to needs that will cross departmental and agency boundaries. There needs to be recognition that just as families live their lives 'in the round', so, too, must services be holistic in their orientation and fit together in an integrated fashion. This whole child/whole system approach ensures that the effectiveness of any particular service benefits from being reinforced and complemented by other services working together, for and with children and their parents. Health, education and social care services need to synchronise their efforts. While a nominated lead agency may be appropriate in a particular case, each agency also has a responsibility to articulate and act on its own goals in regard to the shared outcomes, and be clear as to how it can demonstrate that this is being done.

Government departments actively working together on policy can ensure a clearer focus and more accurate targeting of services. Such whole system working can also make for more cost-effective delivery through avoiding duplication, combining impact and getting synergy through the sharing of information and the cross-fertilisation of ideas. Confusion and duplication can be reduced and more impact achieved to ensure good outcomes for children. Integration needs to occur at the policy level in order to set the strategic direction for planning and commissioning, so that opportunities are provided for conjoint, intersectoral and interagency working.

The strategic direction of services being advocated here cannot be achieved without clear assignment of departmental responsibilities. This requires leadership at the apex of government – in the UK this means at Cabinet Office level. Recognition must be given to the specific requirements and differences between those services that are universal and those that are tightly targeted, between those that are supportive and those that are custodial. Each will have its own policy and organisational focus and concerns. However, these must be supplemented by partnership structures and a shared strategic pursuit of primary developmental family support.

Central government cannot, and should not, attempt to direct the day-to-day judgements and activities of staff providing services and support to families. It is, however, essential that staff at all levels play their role in delivering on the strategic direction and standards of service that the government sets out to promote family support. Staff commitment and engagement are vital to developing, mobilising and sustaining the policy community, networks and constituency for change required to deliver developmental family support. Similarly, policy must make it clear that family support services do not exist as an alternative to the care and concern that generally only families and communities can provide in a sustained and effective manner. The goal of state policy should be to engage, complement, reinforce and extend the capacity of families and communities – to draw them into the policy community, promoting family support and recognising their role as self-advocates in policy networks.

CONCLUSION

Policy requires constant monitoring and review at both national and local levels. This should draw on the experience and views of operational managers and frontline staff within both the statutory and voluntary sectors and consultation with children, young people and their families and communities. One aspect of ensuring that everyone involved in children's services is pulling in the same direction is to develop a shared language, one that can be used not only by those inside a policy community but across the networks and within the broader constituency for change. This shared language is not in opposition to the particular perspectives and specialist terms associated with the different occupations and professions. It is a basic language for sharing and reflecting on how agreed goals and activities are being developed and implemented. It also provides the language with which to ask three key reflective questions, each of which generates its sub-questions:

- Is there a constituency for change committed to family support?

  » How is family socially constructed and what are the major changes under way?

  » What indicators, positive and negative, are there of the changes needing to be managed?

- » What are the traditional relationships between the state and the family, including the role of mediating institutions, such as religion and the media?

- » What is the role of NGOs and intergovernmental agencies?

- » What are the major drivers of change – culture, history, economics or politics?

- » What is the political climate and capacity? Is there already a platform of services in place?

- » What is the balance between the government, NGOs and international agencies?

- Is there a clear alignment between policy on family support and the thrust of other economic and social policies?

  - » How is collaboration between departments managed to ensure a 'whole child/whole system' policy framework?

  - » What are the set of indicators against which to measure the achievement of high-level outcomes?

  - » Does the policy promote a combination of targeted services within universal services?

  - » Is there clarity over which department has lead responsibility for which outcomes?

  - » Is a 'levels of need and service' model explicitly promoted by policy?

  - » Is the policy needs-led and inclusive of all children, regardless of age, gender, income, ability, ethnicity or geographical location?

- Is the family support policy coherent, integrative, participatory and sustainable?

  - » Does the policy framework include support and resources for research and information systems?

» Are these outcomes achievable and measurable?

» How can policy build sustainable capacity within social networks to care for children?

» Is there a strong community development foundation to policy and planning?

» Is the policy climate encouraging of innovation in supporting families?

» What are the structures and processes in place to facilitate participation by children and families in policy development and implementation?

» Does the policy recognise and promote the importance of combining the provision of formal services to families with facilitating support to families through informal social networks?

Armed with the answers to these questions and Hardiker and her colleagues' modelling, it becomes possible to not just strategise in support of a preferred form of family support, but to identify the actors within government and the policy community, as well as in the wider, looser networks that will need to be mobilised in a constituency for change.

— Chapter Three —

MANAGING AND LEADING IN FAMILY SUPPORT

INTRODUCTION

Chapter Two framed family support as a political and policy choice – resulting in various constellations of family support, whether these are primarily informally sourced and dependent on family, friends and community networks, or formally organised and professionally led, or some combination of these. The focus here is on family support delivered through a formally organised service, project or programme. Our intention in this chapter is to address the question: what should a well-planned and managed family support service look like? In doing so we consider how the goal of such a service would be realised, and also the key question of what is distinctive about a family support approach to organising and managing a service. We concentrate here on three main dimensions:

- planning and design

- governance structures and processes

- leading and managing.

We recognise that vast swathes have been written on each of these themes, and direct the reader to these literatures for the fundamentals (Buchanan and Huczynski 2007; Coulshed *et al.* 2006; Crosby and Bryson 2005; Kettner 2013; Lawler and Bilson 2010). Here we focus on aspects of organisation and management that are embedded in a family support orientation. We explore the value of logic modelling and theories of change as planning approaches to family support, and what can be gleaned from the new hybrid academic/policy field of implementation science. We also draw on current literature in the field of management and leadership, which privileges the need for an externally directed approach to governance and leadership, embodied in the ideas of the 'post-modern organisation' and the 'boundary-spanning leader'. These align well with the family support policy emphasis on the 'whole child' and integrated working, and running through the chapter are references to how family support principles are central to successful organisations and interventions. The last section elaborates on a number of key concerns for frontline managers – ensuring staff wellbeing and preventing burnout, connecting supervision and reflective practice, and focusing on relationships. The chapter includes an empirically based model for family support management (see Figure 3.3 later).

PLANNING AND DESIGN

Family support interventions start with a concern with needs and rights. Such interventions can be conceived at the policy level, and move from there towards implementation at the local level, or they can be organic, emergent responses to needs, identified and understood locally by ordinary citizens or practitioners, in turn influencing the macro-policy level. Whatever their provenance within a fluid policy world, it is not a new insight that the long-term development and sustainability of interventions requires a planned approach, underpinned by evidence. In thinking about evidence in and for family support services, the ideas of evidence-based and evidence-informed practice are key. Evidence-based practice initially emerged from within medicine. According to Sackett *et al.*:

> Evidence based health care is the conscientious, explicit and judicious use of current best evidence in making decisions regarding the care of individuals. (1996, p.71)

Most often evidence-based practice is thought of as involving evidence from experimental research, either single studies or meta-analysis, that combine experimental studies on the same topic. The key metric in such studies is an effect size, a statistically derived summary number that allows an overall assessment of the value of an intervention or set of interventions. An evidence-informed approach is more broad-based and inclusive of other dimensions. Petr and Walter (2005) usefully set out the idea of evidence-informed best practice being multidimensional. For these authors, evidence-informed practice must be based on quantitative and qualitative sources of data, and must incorporate the wisdom of consumers of services and of professionals. The sources and quality of all of this data are then analysed, resulting in new knowledge. Starting from a clear articulation of values (e.g., as might be reflected in the principles for family support), this new knowledge is used to critique existing practice, leading, in turn, to practice improvement. It should be obvious that this general orientation to thinking about evidence informs the account of planning for family support outlined here, given the commitment to the voices of service users and its commitment to a value base.

Building on a commitment to evidence, two general approaches in social services planning have gained ground in the policy and service landscape in recent years. The first involves using a 'logic model' approach, which is:

> ...a graphic display or 'map' of the relationship between a program's resources, activities and intended results, which also identifies the program's underlying theory and assumptions. (Kaplan and Garrett 2005, p.167)

Logic modelling involves detailed planning processes, whereby the start point is the outcomes that are intended by the intervention, reflecting the underlying need of children and parents (the focus of Hardiker *et al.*'s thinking), and involves collective planning work towards establishing what activities will be required to achieve these and the resources, or inputs, required. Figure 3.1 sets out a fictitious example of a logic model to address problems facing children transitioning from primary to post-primary school, often a key concern facing family support staff intervening in the context of multiple disadvantage.

In this model, the outcomes of awareness, support levels and preparedness are intended by the implementation of four programmes targeting the transitioning children themselves, their parents and older peers already in post-primary education. Underpinning the activities are financial and human resources, as well as procedural and organisational structures. The arrival at such a model requires data generation and research that feeds into relationship-based processes of discussion and negotiation among key stakeholders. These discussions and negotiations focus not only on the desired outcomes, but also on the existence and nature of any barriers to achieving them, the underpinning causes and possible solutions, as well as the roles of stakeholders in creating solutions.

Inputs	Activities	Outputs	Outcomes
1. Programme material costs	1. In primary school activity-based preparation programme	1. Number of participation children	1. New primary school students:
2. Staff costs for summer programme and in school work	2. Targeted information for parents	2. Number of preparation sessions completed with fidelity	more aware of challenges in post-primary school
3. Committee comprising relevant primary and post-primary staff	3. Summer programme with parents and children	3. Number of summer programme sessions completed	more prepared for challenges
4. Agreements on information sharing	4. Older peer mentoring programme	4. Number of parents participating in summer programme	have reliable older peer to provide support
		5. Number of parents receiving information	2. Parents more informed and supportive of children

Figure 3.1: Logic model example

A theory of change approach operates in a similar logical style. Theory of change is most associated with evaluation theory, whereby Carole Weiss proposed that evaluations should be grounded in programmes' theories of change on the assumption that 'social programmes are based on explicit or implicit theories on how and why the program will work' (Weiss 1995, p.66). Like logic modelling approaches, this involves thinking about goals/outcomes, activities and so on, but theory of change approaches imply greater attention to making explicit *why* we can expect activities to lead to outcomes, either in the immediate or longer term. Here, planning involves greater attention to identify 'causality' in advance and testing this through evaluation processes. Theory of change approaches make explicit the theoretical basis and causal assumptions of an intervention that may be more implicit in logic model approaches. For the intervention approach set out in the foregoing logic model, a theory of change approach might reflect social support as one core theory, with the causal effect rooted in its protective and stress-buffering dimensions (Thompson 2015). We prefer the theory of change approach as our overall orientation to service planning for two reasons. First, it can be seen as a broader and more theoretically driven approach to planning for and understanding change than logic modelling. For example, it fits well with one of the core messages of this book, that family support is about the management of change. Second, a theory of change approach can incorporate the benefits of logic modelling as a technique for making explicit the causal assumptions and how they are being harnessed in a process of change – logic modelling becomes a technical tool for planning within an overall theory of change approach.

One criterion for a good logic model is that it should aim to be testable. In this sense, logic models offer ready-made platforms for evaluation as they provide clarity on assumptions about needs, a detailed account of what is needed by way of resources and activities, a sense of immediate, medium and long-term outcomes, the theory of change that can be tested, and the underpinning theoretical concepts that inform that intervention. From a research and evaluation perspective, it removes the need for a phase of interpreting and understanding an intervention before a research design can be established and implemented.

Building from the idea of a general increase in knowledge about planned intervention is the idea that quite a lot is proven about how to intervene with children and families, but that there is a failure in the dissemination and uptake of this knowledge and/or a failure in the implementation of programmes. Thus, programme developers haven't been good at 'scaling up' interventions, and those implementing proven programmes haven't been good at implementing them. Like its cousin, evidence-based practice, implementation science finds its beginnings and dominant content in the health sciences. Thus, those developing the *Journal of Implementation Science* define implementation research as:

> ...the scientific study of methods to promote the systematic uptake of research findings and other evidence-based practices into routine practice, and, hence, to improve the quality and effectiveness of health services. It includes the study of influences on healthcare professional and organisational behaviour. (Eccles and Mittman 2006, p.1)

Transposing this to the social field, the argument goes that there is a need to similarly apply a scientific approach to the study of the implementation of evidence-based practice, so that the full benefits, from programmes and practices that have been proven according to rigorous social science research, can be achieved for children, parents and communities.

However, there is an inherent 'messiness' in planning processes that highly structured and neat frameworks will not reflect. Logic models run the risk of reification – the idea that the plan is the reality, rather than an attempt to reflect a pathway to a possible reality. So, for example, the often challenging processes underpinning the development of a logic model may not be apparent in the graph and associated texts. What can be fitted on to an A4 page in the smallest possible font size can hardly be the basis for the full representation of a social intervention. Related to this is the point that logic models reflect the difference between human and inanimate systems. They reflect what we would like to achieve in an ideal world, our assumptions about the nature of the world, and our understandings of the causal chains we hope exist, linking our planned activities, the contexts within which they are set and the outcomes we hope to achieve. However, logic models don't have the same predictability of non-human systems governed by laws of physics and chemistry, so we can never be certain how the mechanisms of our policies and interventions will operate, how they will be affected by their environments, or their ultimate effectiveness in achieving the outcomes intended. Planning for family support must be viewed as operating within an open system (Katz and Pinkerton 2003b), while not being paralysed by the possibility that currently unknown factors will influence the implementation of services or interventions, or the possibility of currently unknown or unintended consequences from them. The notion of family support as an open system within a global context is explored in more detail later, in Chapter Six.

Reflecting the earlier discussion on evidence-based and evidence-informed practice, the complexity of the planning process is also reflected in a genuine tension between types of evidence – that derived from the scientific literature, or expert knowledge, and that embodied in the experiences of ordinary citizens and practitioners, who are, after all, experts in their own lives. We suggest that this is ever present, ongoing and unresolvable – what matters is that it is acknowledged and negotiated. This applies to both the generation of knowledge required on the nature of the unmet need *and* the unachieved right, required for effective planning, and to the identification of plausible interventions. A community member may not have the conceptual and methodological language on social support theory, but they will be able to give an example of this theory in practice in a way that can make it meaningful in the context of the intervention. A further challenge to theory of change and logic modelling approaches is that planning rarely happens in 'green field' contexts. There are usually extant service infrastructures, funding arrangements and relationships – good and bad – between and among agencies and communities. Planning processes can become sites of struggle for power, priority and resources – service contexts are rarely funding-rich, so organisational survival can mean competing rather than collaborating with fellow service providers.

Yet one of the strengths of the logic modelling approach to planning is that the evidence of the nature of the need, and of the proposed logic of the intervention, is transparent, and the emergent model at least offers the opportunity to question and challenge. One way to strengthen these approaches to planning is to use them flexibly. For example, there could be different versions of the same logic models reflecting changes over time, such as changes within an intervention and its ecology. While not ideal from a research and evaluation point of view, since it creates a 'moving target', thinking of programme logic model versions or iterations may be more useful to managers and staff in services. Adopting a flexible approach would also reflect the reasonable assumption that services improve in the process of implementation, and feeding back learning on intervention strengths and weaknesses through these processes. Thus, while we endorse the need for good planning underpinned by theories, models and frameworks to guide family support, this must be allied to 'in practice' experience and allow room for manoeuvre.

Family support and logic modelling/theory of change approaches might seem to be strange bedfellows at first glance. The foundations of these technocratic service planning models, within a positivist, objective social science frame, are in many ways at odds with the relational, subjective and critical dimensions of a family support approach. Our argument in favour of their inclusion within a family support approach to management rests on the value of being rigorous in planning, implementing and evaluating family support, and the role of logic modelling and theory of change in achieving such rigour. The role of family support theories and principles within services and interventions is named, made transparent and open to analysis in systematic approaches to planning. Balancing the abstract rigour is the concrete rigour of creating the conditions for relationship-based practice that have to underpin any successful family support intervention.

GOVERNANCE STRUCTURES AND PROCESSES

To function, survive and sustain, even the smallest organisations need to have governance structures and processes. In the main, these are internally focused and relate to planning, finance, human resources and so on. Increasingly they must also allow the organisation to engage effectively with the external environment. In recent years, there have been significant changes in how public and voluntary service organisations are conceptualised, with models and frameworks emerging that reflect themes of flexibility and integration – the cupped model of family support strongly reflects these themes (see Figure 1.2 in Chapter One). These changes reflect the emphasis in policy research on the idea of 'wicked' problems. As implied, these are the types of problems that have complex underpinning causes, and often even more complex possible solutions, requiring joint work between various organisations (Devaney and Spratt 2009).

In her work on evaluating leadership in community interventions concerned with 'wicked' problems, Ozan (2014) identifies Williams (2002) as a key theorist, particularly in his work on traditional and post-modern organisations and leadership and on 'boundary spanners'. Williams suggests that traditional management and organisational structures are not suited to solving 'wicked' problems, and invokes the idea of post-modern organisational forms and approaches. Broadly, such governance approaches emphasise inter- rather than intra-organisational issues, and are concerned with relationships, interconnections and interdependencies rather than linear, rational approaches. For post-modern management structures, important themes are holistic approaches, partnership and networking, which contrast with themes of professionalism, autonomy and compartmentalism associated with traditional organisational forms (Williams 2002, p.105).

While not accepting the post-modernist label with its associated assumptions about contemporary economic, social and cultural phenomena (Callinicos 1991), from a family support perspective, the framing of needs and responses set out as principles in Chapter

One aligns well with the idea of 'wicked' problems and the need for flexible organisational forms with more agile, creative, enabling leadership. In particular, such an organisational approach sits well with core elements of the definition of family support and its principles, for example child-centred, integrated and partnership work, breadth of provision, multi-access referral paths and flexibility and responsiveness in provision.

Williams goes on to suggest a contrast between the leadership approach in modern and post-modern organisations.

Here 'post-modern' leadership involves a facilitative, collaborative approach, with an emphasis on being a catalyst for change, not seeking to 'own' solutions and recognising different ways of solving problems. This contrasts with modern approaches which emphasise hierarchical approaches; heroic leadership that 'takes charge' and 'provides the right answers' (Williams 2002, p.112). Linked to the enabling leadership role is the 'boundary spanner' role (see Figure 3.2). Williams (2013, p.19) characterises boundary spanners as:

> ...individuals who have a dedicated job role or responsibility to work in collaborative environments...who co-ordinate, facilitate and service the processes of collaboration between a diverse set of interests and agencies.

In his conception, boundary spanners can operate at senior or frontline levels.

As seen in Figure 3.2, Williams identifies three core competencies – reticulist, entrepreneur and interpreter – each of which has ready application to family support roles (Williams 2010, p.11). More recently, Williams (2013) has argued that while there will always be those within the public sector focused on specialised areas relevant only to their own organisation, for those charged with working in collaborative settings, competency in boundary spanning has to be part of the general skills set.

A further dimension of governance in family support provision is participation, a well-established imperative for organisations serving children and families, and a key principle identified earlier in Chapter One. Within family support organisations

Roles and competencies

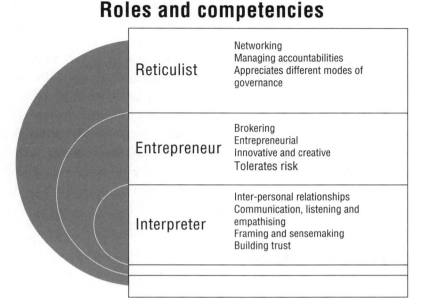

Figure 3.2: Boundary spanner roles and competencies

and interventions, it must be a defining feature, with genuine commitment to involving parents in meaningful, non-tokenistic ways. Such involvement can be focused at the individual child, young person or case level, reflecting both equality commitments (equal valuing of the knowledge and role of children and parents in solutions to problem-solving to that of professionals), and as a strategic focus on resilience building (the long-term value to a person of managing the changes within their own life including leading the necessary problem-solving).

Participation also needs to be a dimension of governance – involving parents and children in the operating processes (planning, recruitment, service design, quality assurance/evaluation) and/ or in structures – for example, in the overall governance of specialist subcommittees. The focus here is on democracy and citizen participation, themes elaborated on in Chapter Two earlier, but again with the possibility of impact at an individual level for parents and children. Within the child protection and welfare field, there are various examples of how this might be done, inclusive of advisory fora, service user committees linked to service design and participation in recruitment processes for personnel, among others (Kennan, Brady and Forkan 2016). What is less evidenced is the impact of these approaches, individually or collectively. Research by Thomas and Percy-Smith on the Children in Care Councils (CiCCs) highlights some positive effects for participating children, but also identifies problems, for example a lack of real power in the CiCCs, and the view of their informants of a need to embed a wider culture of participation in their structures (Thomas and Percy-Smith 2012). If staff and managers don't have the required commitment and skills to achieve meaningful involvement of children and parents as partners, participatory structures and processes will be merely tokenistic.

LEADING AND MANAGING

From a developmental family support management perspective, having a well-functioning staff team is essential. This section describes the components that enable such conditions for the workforce on an overriding assumption that staff are fully focused on meeting the needs of children and parents and upholding a child rights perspective. Rather than seeing this focus on children's needs and rights as 'rhetoric', for any manager of a family support service it is the professional compass by which to judge success or failure at a most basic level. Highlighted earlier in Chapter One, this is also the pinnacle point within the cupped model for family support.

Getting the culture of a family support service right so that it is proactive for children and families and fully supportive of its staff is vital, as is enabling the condition for the family support service to continue to function at an optimal level. Mor Barak, Nissly and Levin (2001), in their meta-analysis of research on reasons for staff leaving service organisations, highlighted the components of poor culture and itemised factors for consideration by child welfare management as follows:

- burnout

- job dissatisfaction

- availability of employment alternatives (mentoring to alternative careers)

- low organisational and professional commitment

- lack of social support.

While Mor Barak *et al.* (2001) found these to be the strongest predictors of turnover or intention to leave, from family support management it could be argued that each of these five negative factors could be restructured more positively as part of an intent to create a positive culture. For example, measuring job satisfaction among frontline staff by management with a view to enhancing work commitment and fulfilment could in itself enable a more conducive work culture and environment.

From a management perspective, having a well-supported staff team is more likely to yield better coping and better practice, as well as increasing the likelihood of better outcomes for the children and families they work with. While not novel, it should serve as a constant reminder to all stakeholders. Over a decade ago a specially commissioned state study of effective family support services in Ireland highlighted the fact that services were deemed to be more effective where frontline staff were given ample support. Additionally the study found that in such conditions the service was more likely to produce a workforce who contribute more fully to the young people, parents and communities they work with and for (Brady, Dolan and Canavan 2004). This research established a set of key operating principles as core to effective management:

- a range of services is available, targeted at different levels of need, within a framework of prevention

- services have clear objectives and a management and organisational culture that facilitates their achievement

- the service has a culture of learning and development

- the service measures outcomes

- the service has adequate resources to meet its objectives and offers value for money

- the service has a commitment to effective partnership practice

- services provide good staff development and support.

Assuming that these guiding management principles are operational in any service and at any point in time, the wider range of functional and operational activities of any family support service are more likely to flourish. These multiple factors are represented in the outer ring of Figure 3.3, a model for developmental family support, and include aspects such as staff that are interested and able, with a commitment to partnership, working internally and externally. This being the case, it also affords better practice principles to flourish, as indicated in the inner ring of Figure 3.3, and relates to intervention-level principles including a whole child focus, and responsive, effective work practices. Finally, this model of management and intervention-level principles, coupled with the ten family support practice principles (highlighted earlier in Chapter One), measured through the central hub and spokes method, provides a strong general road map for family support management.

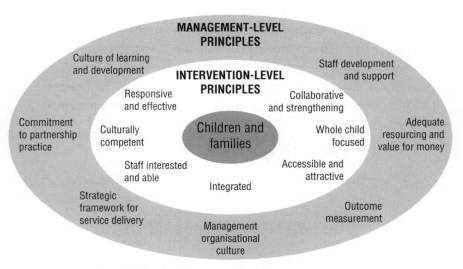

Figure 3.3: A model for developmental family support management

Focusing on the individual staff member, effective supervision, which is goal-orientated and task completion or solution-orientated, is key to supporting staff working in family support (Davis and Smith 2012). This is inclusive of models whereby staff are constructively challenged on their practice and, ideally, where service user direct feedback is incorporated into planning towards improving work practice (Frost *et al.* 2015). Crucially good supervision has to be regular and fulsome, not just in times of crisis management (Morrison 2009). Effective supervision should also ensure the ongoing capacity to allow the donor and recipient of supervision ample opportunity to work on meeting needs and upholding the rights of children and parents (Moran, Ghate and van der Merwe 2004).

Just as frontline staff need regular supervision in order to keep functioning well in their work, it is equally important for managers themselves to be in receipt of high-quality supervision. In some cases, having an external supervisor for managers helps and is more effective than 'in house' provision. First, it enables better objectivity, particularly in times of particular stress for managers, staff and those who are using the family support service. Second, externally sourced supervision can offer managers a wider perspective and solutions based on the experience of others facing similar work issues.

It has been argued in earlier work (Dolan *et al.* 2006) that effective supervision and robust use of reflective practice go hand in hand. Using methods of reflective practice, whereby staff think in action on their actions (i.e. reflect on what they are doing while they are doing it), can enhance the quality of supervision (Thompson 2012). Similarly, robust models of supervision allow the opportunity for staff to be and become more reflective in their work. One of the ways of bringing supervision and reflective practice together can involve three distinct goals and have particular resonance for family support management. First, ensuring a strengths-based perspective inclusive of the views and wishes as well as agency of service users should be central to supervision considerations and self-reflective processes. Second, mutual goal-setting for supervision and reflective practice can be helpful to both the manager and frontline worker alike (Morrison 2000). This includes questions such as, what is urgent and immediate that has to be addressed swiftly? What are the medium-term issues for consideration, and what are the longer-term goals (over months or a year) that need to be considered and worked on? And third, opportunities for staff to flourish, take the initiative, develop new ways of working and newer solutions to dealing with difficult practice tasks that can be shared with colleagues should be fostered.

At a wider level the importance of good multidisciplinary and interagency working in child protection and welfare has been well established over recent decades (Munro, Taylor and Bradbury-Jones 2013). The importance for management in ensuring staff are well connected to other professionals and services is not just desirable, but essential. Where the importance of interagency working in child protection has been highlighted (all too often after tragic failure in terms of child maltreatment), its importance in terms of family support has been less emphasised. However, in the context of strengths-based working, having social support enlistment and resilience building working 'in concert' is equally key (Dolan 2012).

Similarly, just as the need to work across the social ecology of a child and family has been highlighted as key within a systems working perspective, working across the service ecology through link-up work is also of particular importance. In a family support context this is most notable for three distinct reasons. First, it requires a move away from turf war service provision mentality or the mythical belief that managers see their agency as working far harder than all other agencies, operating in a context of a 'siege' mentality. Second, and conversely, it requires a true belief in parity of esteem across professionals and a move away from an insinuation of a pecking order of importance, whereby some are seen as of more importance and status than others (Ferguson

2010). It could be argued, particularly in a family support context, that those who work most directly day in day out with children and parents should, if anything, be given pole position in discussion among professionals in relation to family and practice interventions. Finally, in relation to connectivity in family support, the importance of children, young people, parents and other family voices should be seen as part of multidisciplinary working and a crucial source of important information to managers of services. Simple triangulation of the voice of the child/parent, fellow professionals external to the service and the views of frontline staff should form the basis for ensuring accuracy in terms of assessment, design and implementation of interventions and assurance in terms of impact of family support work.

The volume of demand on a service, coupled with a lack of resources, can be particularly challenging for managers. This is particularly the case in family support, where often, despite the success of both staff and the service, due to financial constraints services are either not allowed to grow or, worse, are the subject of cutbacks. Certainly, there are often conditions where family support is placed below the assumed priority of other service functions, for example child protection.

Regardless of these circumstances and stresses, managers must retain the capacity not to spread a service so wide in order to reach many at the cost of either poor or bad practice. In family support it is better to ensure staff work well with a limited number of children and families than poorly or ineffectively with many. There is an onus on managers to show duty of care to children, young people and parents. Similarly, managers need to show the same attention to frontline staff who, if over-burdened, will inevitably suffer burnout and need to leave. The distinct difference between staff being unable rather than unwilling to provide effective family support can be a thin one in the context of an overworked service and workforce (Devaney 2013). Ensuring that there are adequate staff in a service along with adequate resources is a basic but crucial requirement of effective family support management (Whittaker

2009). Similarly, for the workforce, the assumption that newly qualified staff, who are typically younger, are the ones always in need of mentoring and professional development should not be taken as given by service management. There are young and new staff with innate wisdom who will effectively support children and parents way beyond their years of experience through professional skills. Similarly there are veterans of practice who struggle and for whom professional development, including refresher training, can be key, and who may need a new lease of development in their practice skills (Buckley, Carr and Whelan 2010).

Even where there are ample resources and staff, success in family support management should include two core considerations. First, there are constantly new programmes to support families either being pilot tested, introduced post-evaluation, scaled up or modified. Some of these are freely available and some are simply not affordable. While such programmes are often helpful and well worthy of consideration for implementation, they still do not and cannot overtake the importance of basic relationships between frontline staff and those with whom they work. As far back as the early 1980s Whittaker and Garbarino (1983) neatly defined this as the core issue of supporting families, and described it as the 'bread and butter of relationships'. This suggests that while programmes are important and helpful in family support, as identified internationally by 'veterans' of family support, people are more and most important (Devaney and Dolan 2012). Similarly, just as we manage services to produce better outcomes through what are labelled proven programmes, we similarly need to ensure that the relationships with those we work with and for not just exist but enable coping, a foundation for effective family support.

CONCLUSION

A set of 'active' family support management practice questions emerge for those planning and overseeing the delivery of services, including the following:

- Are theory of change and logic model approaches used in planning services? In their application, is a balance sought between underpinning science, citizens' knowledge of their lives and practitioners' experience?

- In implementing evidence-based programmes, is attention to intervention fidelity balanced with responsive practice that meets need as it presents?

- Are the underpinning theories in family support explicit in intervention logic models/theories of change?

- Are governance and leadership structures and processes outward-looking, reflective of the idea that the service will be one part of a holistic solution to complex problems? Do multidisciplinary and multiagency activities in which the intervention is involved reflect strengths-based approaches? Are they orientated towards enlisting social support and building resilience?

- Is an outward-looking 'boundary-spanning' dimension in leadership and/or individual roles of staff complementing the core business of the organisation or intervention?

- What appropriate and meaningful opportunities are there for children, young people and parents to participate in governance structures and processes? Are these being validated through ongoing monitoring of their value at individual and group levels and for the organisation?

- Do service managers and leaders actively reflect on whether the necessary conditions are in place for the delivery of effective management support?

- How is the staff team being supported and sustained? What role does supervision have? Do supervision approaches incorporate the use of reflective practice?

- Is the staff team being supported to make relationship building and maintenance the central plank of day-to-day practice?

— Chapter Four —

DIRECT WORK WITH CHILDREN, PARENTS AND COMMUNITIES

INTRODUCTION

This chapter considers direct work with children, parents and communities. The intention is to provide an overview of the 'diverse "tool kit" of skills and approaches' (Frost *et al.* 2015, p.3) available for the varying contexts in which family support is provided directly to children and young people, and their parents, friends and neighbours. The ecological context of the family environment in which family support is delivered must be seen as a crucial part of direct work, whatever the precise target of the work. As has been well established, no family problems occur in isolation, and the wider social environment needs consideration, not only as a contributory factor to deficits and difficulties, but also as a source of potential strengths and solutions. Direct work interventions should not occur without consideration of the influences of the wider social ecology – in particular, for direct family support work, the micro- and meso-systems that make up the top three tiers of the cupped model of social ecology (see Figure 1.2 in Chapter One).

This chapter is not an encyclopaedic description of each and every type of programme or intervention in family support. Rather, it seeks to provide an overall sense of the practice landscape, emphasising those features that are central to the form of strengths-based, inclusive and empowering family support being argued for in this book. The importance of enlisting and mobilising social support to reinforce and build resilience as a key component of direct work is emphasised. Related to this, relationship-based working is presented as the heart of direct work. In this regard, we advocate an emphasis on ongoing reflective practice inclusive of empathic action as a key tool in self-regulation for professionals engaged in working directly with children, young people, parents and communities. Finally, the implications of the ten family support principles set out in Chapter One are considered in order to establish a set of key reflective questions for direct work with children, parents and communities.

ENLISTING SOCIAL SUPPORT

At its most basic level, enabling children, young people and families to cope and thrive is contingent on the provision and enlistment of social support. In the first instance, this involves assessment of support needs by establishing the sources, types, amounts and qualities of help on offer to an individual or family. Typically, types of support include:

- concrete – the practical acts of assistance between people to undertake specific tasks and achieve particular goals

- emotional – comprising acts of empathy, listening and generally 'being there' for another person

- advice – a combination of information giving and sharing judgements, which can be as much about comfort and reassurance as new thinking

- esteem – centring on how one person respects another's worth and communicates that to them.

Sources of support can be informal (unpaid) help such as from extended family, friends or neighbours, semi-formal help from volunteers (possibly financially supported) or formal help from paid professionals. Informal sources of help are key to family support and yet can all too easily be overlooked by professionals. They are mistakenly judged to be unavailable either because family members, friends and neighbours are assumed unwilling to support or are judged to be lacking in adequate skills and capacity. In general, most people prefer to use natural sources of help in a crisis because it is more widely available, not constrained by office hours, and can be reciprocated in a way that lessens the sense of being beholden. The 'buffer to stress' role of natural family support has been well established (see Dolan and Brady 2012). In recent years, the importance of hidden support (assistance received anonymously) or help that is provided in very discreet ways has been found to be a better form of supportive action (Bolger and Amarel 2007). Similarly, the importance of understanding the quality of these social networks and how they work rather than just who is in them has also been highlighted as a key aspect of family support. So it is not only about who is there to help that matters, but rather, what type of assistance, how often, how much, and in what exact ways a person will donate their support that counts.

It is crucially important that professionals engaging with families recognise that it is within the family and its network that the resources for significant and sustained change lies. An awareness by professionals of the value of informal and natural sources of support as part of face-to-face working is key. However, there is also a risk that professionals who use natural social support networks in order to assist the families they work with may overestimate the availability of natural help on offer. For example, professionals may overlook that, over time, the burden of caregiving can exasperate the supporter to a point of burnout, leading to any supply of help 'drying up'. Similarly, the conditions under which a natural supporter can provide assistance may alter at any time due to life events or other multiple pressing demands. The sister who helped the stressed single parent with regular babysitting and occasional financial support may find that this starts to create difficulties in her own family following her partner becoming unemployed, leading to her support tailing off. This may occur unbeknownst to the set of professionals working with the family who were not aware of it in the first place and so cannot calibrate the level and type of their support accordingly. Finally, social support is key when it is delivered via interventions and programmes that offer support in normal times as well as periods of stress. Ensuring children, young people and parents have access to ample instrumental and emotional support, which is dependable and reciprocal, should be a key focus of all direct work.

FAMILY SUPPORT PRACTICE LANDSCAPE

Ahead of any exploration of family support programmes, formal direct work interventions, or the expected and desired outcomes characteristic of the different models of family support discussed in Chapter Two (see Table 2.3), the basic needs of children and their carers requires attention. Many families experience as part of their everyday life very real material deprivation and the stigma and social exclusion that can accompany it (Daly and Kelly 2015). For those engaged in family support, all too easily 'poverty can become the "wallpaper" that is clearly visible but seldom considered' (Welbourne 2012, p.114). Not just individual families but certain populations, such as Roma children and adults, are socially excluded and in need of basics, such as food, clothing and shelter (World Bank 2015). With the global and economic downturn following the financial crisis of 2008, for many families the most important direct family support intervention includes food transfers and food banks in order for them to survive at the most basic human level. This form of direct intervention and provision for children, young people and parents needs to be given recognition as a first and basic need and as a fundamental form of family support, which overrides in priority any formal programmes provided by professionals and services.

Asserting the importance of provision addressing very basic needs being recognised as family support is part of ensuring an inclusive view of the field. Whereas there may be a perception that the development of early intervention and prevention through family support programmes is a relatively new concept in service provision, this is not the case (Frost *et al.* 2015). What is the case is that in recent years there has been a growth in the use of tightly designed and tested programmes such as Sure Start (Belsky *et al.* 2006; NESS Research Team 2004), Incredible Years (Webster Stratton and Reid 2010) and Triple P-Positive Parenting (Sanders

2012). It is important to note that, prior to this, programmes such as Parent Effectiveness Training (Cedara and Lavant 1990) and the Family Group Conference (Connolly and Masson 2014) had been in existence in many countries.

It would be a mistake to regard only the licensed, evaluated and well-marketed programmes as family support. While such programmes may be prominent, there are also in existence numerous local and regionally developed programmes that have strong value and utility but are just not registered in the literature (Brady *et al.* 2004). Ten years ago in Ireland the Department of Children and Youth Affairs commissioned a review of such lesser-known family support programmes. The review revealed not only just how many of these there were, but also a number of common components in what were deemed by local authorities to be exemplary family support programmes, such as services being open and available at the times that service users needed them most, and staff acting as brokers with other agency staff in other services (Brady *et al.* 2004). It is notable that the key factor identified as central to success was leadership within the service or agency. This was typically provided by a project leader who acted as both advocate and champion for the service and service users alike.

Across both licensed and localised programmes there is also a wide variety of ways in which family support is delivered. They can offer to work individually, one to one with a child, young person or parent, and can provide peer-to-peer mentoring support. They can also provide support through group work. In some programmes a combination of formats is used. There are programmes that focus on children by their stage of development, some that focus on the home, school or community as sites of delivery, and others that target the intervention in terms of type of disadvantage and adversity. Certain projects focus solely on issues of families and poverty, and are most typically area-based within communities designated as deprived. Support services for families living with a disability focus on sustaining and enhancing the lives of not only the disabled person but also other family members, ensuring that they have their rights upheld and have access to full community living experiences (Frost *et al.* 2015).

Many family support programmes are designed as interventions within the micro-system of the family, based on psycho-social 'ages and stages' child development theory, usually, but not always, by psychologists or social workers, and tend to focus on outcomes linked to individual wellbeing (Frost and Dolan 2012; Frost *et al.* 2015). Such services and programmes are implemented on the sequential basis of assessment, intervention, monitoring of progress, evaluation of impact and closure. They may include use of logic models and theories of change. Many are time-limited, are delivered through weekly sessions and target behavioural change on the part of young people and/or their parents. Some are manualised and provide a curriculum typically with session tasks and outcomes. For some there is a very specific focus to the intervention, for example programmes for adolescents with mental health problems. Conversely, others may be orientated to changing chaotic lifestyles in order to prioritise parenting.

Whether family support programmes focus on universal provision, target issues of protection for those at risk or provide services to help compensate for experiences of extreme adversity (Gilligan 2000) will reflect both how need is understood and political choice about state intervention – in other words, according to which model of family support is being followed: primary developmental, secondary institutional or tertiary residual (see Table 2.3 in Chapter Two). Generally there is actually a combination of the models, with one being promoted to set the general ethos of the system. This systemic context can determine whether the same programme is being delivered and experienced by the family as open access and in response to expressed need, being offered as a preventative, early intervention, or as an imposed legally mandated intervention to address child protection concerns.

Typically the universal services associated with the primary developmental approach apply in relation to early years with a view to enabling school readiness. The emphasis on early childhood development and the importance of the first three years of life as key is well known (Heckman 2006). In the UK Sure Start has been acknowledged as a key intervention programme in this regard, with an emphasis on the intellectual and social development of the child

(NESS Research Team 2010). Following this route of 'age and stage'-based services for children during their latency years (between the ages of three and seven), in addition to the role of primary school, sporting and leisure activities, specific family support programmes such as Experience Corps and Wizards of Words are available focusing on literacy support. The Incredible Years programme targets behavioural issues for children in the 5–11 age group by working with children and parents. Many of these programmes focus on positive parenting and include teaching parents skills in managing specific issues. For parents under stress there are new targeted parenting programmes becoming available, such as the suite offered by Parenting NI.[1]

In relation to adolescence, most schools offer social, personal development and health programmes. The provision of programmes in school settings has also increased, and notably so in Ireland; for example, on-site school-based peer-to-peer mentoring (Dolan and Brady 2012). Outside of school many young people can access youth clubs and more targeted youth programmes available to them locally. There are many focused intervention programmes now available including youth mentoring, youth development projects and mental and sexual health initiatives, either based in schools or community settings. For adolescents with particular mental health issues, community adolescent mental health service programmes are becoming increasingly available as the extent of need in this area becomes ever more apparent. Some family support services are totally issues-based in their nature – for example, Alateen supports young people dealing with alcohol addiction in their family.[2] For this age group there are also numerous parenting programmes that are either provided universally by the state, NGOs or faith-based organisations.

In the past, family support services were delivered primarily through home visitation work by social workers, but today, similar to the move towards general practice being delivered in surgeries, there is a move towards local centre-based provision. At the same

---

1   See www.parentingni.org
2   See www.al-anonuk.org.uk/public/what-alateen

time, the number of social workers who undertake direct family support work with families has lessened, with a wide range of para-professionals, including an occupational category titled 'family support worker', now occupying this space. There is a mixed view on whether this has been good for the social work profession (Jack 2015). Apart from domiciliary-based service provision, family support is often provided in community settings, either in a community development project setting or through a more centralised social services centre or community health clinic. For young people their preference is often for services to be delivered outside of the home, and ideally in a non-stigmatising setting. So, for example, the use of youth cafés is popular with young people experiencing adversity including a health concern. In this way they can receive a targeted programme in a universal setting in a discreet manner. The Communities That Care (CTC) programme (Hawkins *et al.* 2008) uses a corporate approach to resolving issues for children and parents through localised but targeted support interventions. The underlying ethos of the programme is that families who have issues should not be segregated or stigmatised. As typically their problems are occurring within their local community, it is the obvious site for seeking and implementing solutions.

There is an obvious element of potential crossover between the various programmes, approaches and domains of family support; for example, the provision of early years services to alleviate stress on a single parent living in a disadvantaged community may exist alongside a community-based service that works with young people with mental health concerns appropriate to the oldest son of the same single parent. Knowing that the two services are there means that interventions can be combined to meet the needs of different members while strengthening the family as a whole.

FAMILY SUPPORT IN ACTION

In undertaking the direct work of providing family support it is useful to consider what is the primary focus, the setting and type of support – developmental, compensatory or protective. This is illustrated in the following three case examples.

Case example 1

Mary is parenting alone with four young children (ranging in age from nine months to six years). She lives in social housing and is dependent on Income Support. She has limited contact with her extended family or with her neighbours. She feels generally under stress, and finds it particularly hard to cope with the behaviour of her eldest daughter. To her regret she has resorted to slapping the child, resulting in visible bruising. Mary has recognised this as her problem, and sought help through her family doctor. Mary is now being visited at home by a family support worker, and is following a parenting programme that includes parenting skills enhancement, including non-violent ways of dealing with child behaviour. In addition, there is close monitoring of protection issues, in this case by both the family support worker and the local child protection worker. So, in terms of family support provision, in this case it is delivered at home, focusing on meeting need in adversity, and is protective in nature (see Figure 4.1).

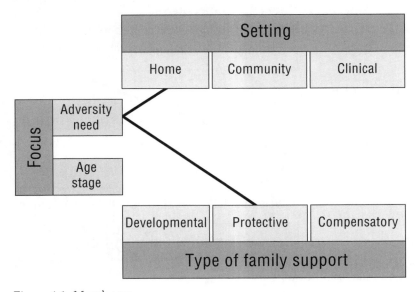

Figure 4.1: Mary's case

Case example 2

Brian, aged six, is a very outgoing boy who lives at home with his parents and attends his local school. Although doing reasonably well in school, Brian has a speech impediment that causes him stress, leaves him vulnerable to bullying, and to some extent is impairing him in terms of school achievement and social interactions with friends and peers. For the last two months Brian has been seeing a speech and language therapist in a local health clinic. After just four weekly sessions at the clinic, in addition to support from his parents at home on voice exercising, Brian is responding very well, and is already showing improvement in terms of his capacity to express himself and in terms of his self-confidence. In this case example the intervention is targeting direct work with a young boy in a clinical setting, focusing on bringing him to an appropriate age/stage in terms of language ability in what is an issue of developmental delay (see Figure 4.2).

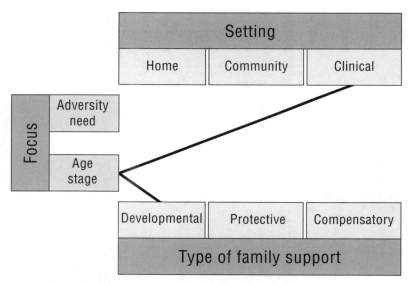

Figure 4.2: Brian's case

Case example 3

David left the care of long-term foster parents aged 17 to start university in another city. While he was in care he had maintained contact with his birth family and continued to do so on leaving care. He also kept in contact with his foster parents. However, he found these family contacts were greatly weakened by his move, and this added to a general sense of social isolation and loneliness. His social worker arranged through the university student support services for a student peer mentor from David's home town. Michael was in his final year and was able to give David practical advice and reassurance about managing both his studies and his social life at university. As they both shared an interest in drama, they volunteered to help with the university drama society production, which helped with David's self-confidence and gave him a circle of university friends. As Michael had a car he was able to provide David with a lift to their home town at holidays so that he could stay with his foster family and visit his birth parents. Figure 4.3 illustrates this case example.

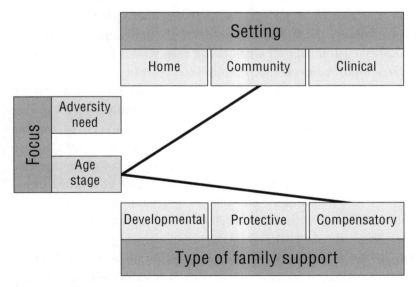

Figure 4.3: David's case

FAMILY SUPPORT PRACTICE

Just as much as the systemic context needs to be recognised as determining the actual experience of family support, the role of the individual worker also needs to be taken into account. Some workers feel more comfortable and are more competent in delivering licensed programmes, while others work more effectively through localised approaches. Both approaches require some 'road map' or 'recipe' to give direction to the work. The difference is one of degree. At one end of the continuum are the licensed programmes that have a manualised 'curriculum for practice', with a step-by-step session guide aimed at securing a predetermined week-by-week incremental progression. To ensure success with such programmes there is a requirement that those delivering them have been formally trained in their use, and that implementation closely follows the instructions, ensuring 'fidelity' to the programme. This approach allows for rigorous evaluation of implementation and licence protection, but can fail to engage with the complexity of families' lives.

At the other end of the continuum are approaches dependent on the use of experience and professional wisdom with the 'relationship' factor, and the detailed individual, family and locality customising of work being seen as more important than curriculum content. Such fluid interventions can play to the strengths of some workers in connecting with families. However, they can be difficult to manage, both for the family support worker and for the agency, with loss of clarity around objectives, making evaluation and decisions about closure difficult. In between the two ends of the continuum there are varying degrees of predetermined intervention; for example, with manuals acting as a guide rather than a rule for workers, and following general practice principles being more important than fidelity to the programme.

There may be times when the strict following of a programme might be the preferred intervention. At other times, where children, young people or parents are particularly vulnerable and finding their capacity to cope very diminished, the supportive relationship factor may be more needed. Conversely, where families are in a strong position to act on their capacity to change and to devise positive new directions for themselves, they should be afforded the opportunity to adapt programmes, access their own sources of support and use their individual agency. This requirement of flexibility may be dependent on nuances of time and circumstances for families; for example, when service users are facing multiple problems at the same point, they may need to take a necessary temporary 'rain check' on a particular intervention. Professionals should not see this as a lack of motivation to engage in a programme, but rather evoke understanding and empathy, in themselves forms of support, for the reality of a family's life at a given time.

Another important element to consider is the role of personal agency on the part of children and young people, and their parents and families. Those who advocate very strongly for greater participation by service users in the assessment, design, implementation and evaluation of family support see the licensed programmes as too restrictive and being imposed. They take the view that if programme objectives and content are already set to such an extent that there is little contribution from those who receive it, this narrows and rules out issues that may need to be addressed, and can lead to a sense of diminished agency and the disempowering of families in thrall of the expert. However, those who advocate for programme fidelity argue that having a proven route to a solution to a problem from a planned intervention is both appealing and empowering to the recipient. Both perspectives need to be taken into account when a worker is considering the approach they feel most confident and competent with, in negotiation with those they intend to work with.

What must not be overlooked is the key factor of the relationship between the supporter and those being supported. Regardless of how strong the evidence base of an intervention may be, the programme does not make the worker. Similarly, the experience and skills of an intuitive worker achieves nothing unless a relationship is established. Relationship is not only the key in regard to licensed and localised formal family support, but also in regard to informal support networks. Family support is about human interactions and people supporting other people, and a core condition for this to be successful lies within the strength, trust and sense of closeness, reciprocity and durability of the relationship between the caregiver and recipient. Within informal systems, trust is the glue of social capital. There is strong evidence that a relationship is also key to successful formal interventions (Howe 1995; Thompson 2009).

At the same time as the importance of a relationship cannot be overstated, neither should the challenge of relationship work be underestimated. Rather than seeing positive relationships as a given, there needs to be recognition that providing support to families requires considerable skills and expertise, and can be exhausting and stressful for the worker. Reflective practice is essential in order to ensure those who provide family support are aware of their professional and personal influence on those they work with (Dolan *et al.* 2006). Reflective practice should encourage an holistic view on the part of the worker by which he or she takes into consideration the elements of programmes, the needs of the person being worked with and the role of all other relevant actors involved. All these need to be considered and viewed as constantly in flux. Recognising this encourages continuous, flexible adjustment that can be thought of as a sponge-like quality to intervention. Just as a sponge can retain or release water but still retain its shape, such flexibility to wax and wane in programme interventions is a crucial aspect of family support.

BUILDING RESILIENCE

Over the last 20 years in particular there has been a growing interest in enabling children and families to demonstrate resiliency as part of their personal process in dealing with adversity. Although the concept of resilience predates this specific aspect of its value, mechanisms by which a young person or parent can thrive in times of extreme difficulty have come much more to the fore. This growing interest can be seen not only in the academic journals (Canavan 2008), but also in manualised family support programmes, and in the creation of research for practice measurement tools (see, for example, the Child and Youth Resilience Measure in Ungar *et al.* 2010). Since the pioneering work in the 1970s, various descriptions for the process of demonstrating resilience have become part of common language for child welfare professionals, such as 'outcomes', 'risk' and 'protective factors'. Resilience can be described as where the risk factors in a young person's life are outweighed by the protective factors; for example, risk of physical harm towards a child from a parent under stress may be outweighed by the protective factor of support to both the child and parent from family and close friends.

It has been argued that within the development of resilience there are 'turning points' or key life moments that enable a person to turn a corner and commence recovery (Gilligan 2009b). Conversely, resilience is also seen to express the power of everyday living, what has been described as 'the power of ordinary magic' (Masten 2014), and processes to enable resilience for a person occur over time rather than being one-off significant events. Similarly, the mundane experiences of life have been highlighted as crucial ongoing aspects of becoming resilient (Gilligan 2008).

The following set of conditions, termed the '5 Rs', need to be present and active in the lives of young people and, if not present and/or consistent, enabled by the professionals who work with and for them: responsibility, respect, reciprocity, ritual and routine. Apart from their importance in helping long-term recovery, all these components should be core to family support direct work and be seen as valued as 'coping enablers' in the present as much as 'resilience builders' in the future.

Similarly, the importance of mastery of leisure interests and hobbies has been identified as a key component of direct work (Gilligan 2009b). Such activities enable mastery for family members and offer them respite from their difficulties and stresses, along with opening new positive relationship opportunities for them and building their self-efficacy. The importance of personal achievement through arts, sport or leisure pursuits should not be overlooked as having too mundane a value to be considered as part of a family support programme. Whether pursued as individual or group activities, the wide range and inclusive nature of leisure activities available to children, young people and parents is worthy of consideration. The only bar is likely to be cost and lack of encouragement.

In recent years there has also been an increasing interest in developments, models and methods for coproduction of services (Davis 2011) by greater partnership with young people and families. Although still emergent, it holds the potential to be and become a key concept in family support practice and provision. Coproduction involves better working on participatory practice methods where there is genuine involvement of young people, parents and their social networks in the assessment of problems, design of interventions and evaluation of implementation. Two examples are particularly pertinent to coproduction in family support practice. First, Family Group Conferences (Connolly and Masson 2014) have been used for many years as a method of allowing young people and their parents and supporters to create their own solutions to their difficulties rather than just have professionals dictate the direction of travel for interventions. Second, the more recent interest in affording young people opportunities to become engaged as civic actors through positive engagement has strong potential as a form of discreet coproduction.

Models of youth leadership and citizenship have been found to be most beneficial to young people who are experiencing problems (Redmond and Dolan 2012). Such leadership includes political, social and economic engagement in their families, schools and communities, and is found to have a number of key benefits. Apart from enhancing their mastery, belonging, independence and generosity, through civic engagement young people get respite from their own difficulties, gain insight into the plight of others who may be experiencing adversity, and gain comfort in the realisation that having problems is not something that just happens to them, and that solutions are possible. Importantly, in the case of both Family Group Conferences and youth civic engagement, the emphasis is on the development of personal agency and positive self-action and determination as key components of practice. By implication it suggests the need for fluidity in work practices by professionals, as suggested earlier in this chapter. Interestingly the role of civic engagement of young people has recently been forwarded as an important tool in enabling resilience in young people experiencing serious difficulties (Dolan 2012; Shaw *et al.* 2014). This includes four forms of civic engagement: political, which is often assumed as the only form of civic participation for children and youth; social, which includes acts of altruism with and for others; economic, including participation in the workforce; and moral or ethical, which includes the demonstration of active empathy.

It should be noted that there are some who now argue that there is a need to move away from seeing resilience as a character trait and by implication only to be addressed through direct one-to-one work, and instead to focus on the social ecological aspects of resilience (Ungar 2012). Similarly, there are others who suggest that there are strong limitations to resilience as a concept (Luthar, Cicchetti and Becker 2000) in that it should focus more on sorting the source of stress than the victim or the oppressed. For example, in the case of a young person being bullied at school over issues of sexuality, rather than just focusing on equipping them with personal coping skills, the emphasis should be on working with the homophobic bully and the wider school issues resulting from a culture of heteronormative oppression (Mishna 2012).

Enabling a service user family and/or community's capacity to demonstrate resilience in times of ongoing or future adversity should be a key objective in direct work. Ensuring that risk factors in the young person or parent's life are counterbalanced by protective factors may require direct worker intervention in the wider networks, while still ensuring that due respect and attention is paid to the capacity of the service user to demonstrate agency and action solutions for themselves. Resilience applies not just in the life of the individual, but also in the context of their social ecology. Similarly, social capital is not a commodity or personal asset that an individual owns, but rather a set of actual or potential strengths within the web of relationships that conditions their life. Direct work that focuses on personal coping should be thought of as strengthening and mobilising bonding social capital. In order to move from getting by to getting ahead, that is to say, from bonding to bridging capital, direct work needs to focus on the enlistment of social support from others. In this way direct work should always be seeking to both enable a service user to identify, use and strengthen personal strengths and self-efficacy and at the same time to strengthen social networks via help from others in their family and community. This requires family support workers to develop their own community development skills and/or to join with others with these skills (Broadhead *et al.* 2008; Forde 2015; Mullender, Ward and Fleming 2013; Popple 2015).

One review of effective community development practice identified a set of practitioner 'habits' that family support workers also need. These are clustered around four levels corresponding to the first three levels of the cupped model shown in Chapter One: the intra-personal/personal level, organisational level, inter/cross-organisational level and community/societal level (Weyers, cited in Forde 2015). The habits at the first level involve workers striving to understand their position within the broader context so that they are able to negotiate the inevitable tensions, contradictions and mixed expectations. They take opportunities to improve and develop their knowledge and skills in order to self-empower as a means to empower others. They attend to self-renewal activities such as self-reflection, maintaining their own support networks and self-care. At the organisational level they prioritise fostering facilitative and supportive relationships within all levels of their employing organisation. For inter/cross-organisational working they build and use partnerships and coalitions using research and opportunities for shared learning underpinned by common values and purpose. At this level they also use management and planning to facilitate stakeholder participation and promote a rights agenda. At the community/societal level, effective community development involves collective problem posing and 'conscientisation' along with facilitating ownership of the process by the community.

MAKING REFLECTION CORE TO FAMILY SUPPORT PRACTICE

The understanding that use of 'self' is a key component in direct casework with children, parents and families has been well established over many decades (Ruch *et al.* 2010). We know that how workers do what they do is of equal importance to what they do, and so is core rather than complementary. Regardless of the strength of any proven or promising intervention, including robust manualisation, 'the programme does not make the worker'. Staff need personal skills to communicate and engage positively and constructively with those they work with, and relationship-based practices are a core component to successful working, particularly with hard-to-reach service users (Lefevre 2010; Winter 2011).

Although it may be assumed that professionals who work in family support operate with an innate capacity to demonstrate a caring capacity towards others, this actually cannot be taken as guaranteed or a given. Some workers only follow the most basic required work practices in dealing with children, young people, parents and communities, whereas others go way beyond what their work contract demands. In the worst cases, where children and young people have been harmed or ill treated by those there to support and care for them, in addition to a general poor or negative work culture, specifically there has been a lack of reflective practices that constructively and routinely challenge staff.

Reflective practice involves a step-by-step process of checking and reorientation, and provides a 'translational' method for applying theory to practice (Dolan 2006). It can be neatly described as 'thinking in action on action(s)' on the part of the frontline worker or local service manager. It relates to self-gauging work practice in respect of implementation and impact of delivery of interventions and relationship-based casework. This requires both self-observation and checking with peers and service users as to the quality and impact of work undertaken. The basis of self-reflection and feedback from others, in particular in relation to specific work practice incidents, involves self-recalibration. This involves combining three core types of knowledge: 'know of' (theory), 'know how' (skills) and 'know to' (practice change based on reflection).

Three specific tools for practice are helpful here: the Social Provisions Scale (SPS), as a means to assess availability of support; the Intervention Matrix Model (IMM), for planning interventions that enable resilience building; and the Self-Appraisal Model (SAM), for promoting a reflective style of working – gauging the effectiveness of support from professionals (Dolan *et al.* 2006). All three directly address key aspects of family support. The SPS is a practice-friendly tool for the identification of a young person's perceived sources, levels, types and qualities of social support, and assesses the potential for the enhancement of responsive social network sources. The IMM focuses on finding ways of building resiliency while working with families on coping. The focus of SAM is to monitor and self-check reflective practice on the part of the worker and service through a self-appraisal process. Table 4.1 illustrates these components and their core functions.

Table 4.1: Selecting tools

Purpose	Instrument	Benefit
Assessment of support need	Social Provisions Scale (SPS)	Measures family support enlistment
Intervention to meet need	Intervention Matrix Model (IMM)	Focuses on coping and resilience building
Evaluation of practice	Self-Appraisal Model (SAM)	Enables reflection on quality of intervention

Source: Modified from Dolan et al. (2006)

A capacity on the part of workers to feel empathy, and more importantly to demonstrate to those they are working with that they do, may seem obvious, but its importance as a key component for good practice cannot be emphasised enough. The role of empathy in the context of reflective practice requires more attention than it tends to get, and particularly so in the context of family support practice. Just as not all children learn empathy as part and parcel of early family life experiences, making the role of teachers, schools and other professionals in supplementing values learned at home crucial, it is not unusual for professionals to need support in sustaining and learning improved modes of empathy in their work with and for others. Methods of empathy can be measured as present and correct in the individual and family, as well as among professionals, and include factors such as:

- knowing our feelings

- having a sense of empathy

- learning to manage our emotions

- repairing emotional damage

- putting it all together: emotional interactivity.

Furthermore, empathy can be judged in very simple ways – for example, we judge each other's capacity to listen. When workers are under stress, this simple skill is vital but can be hard to retain. Workers need to guard against ignoring, and as bad, pretending to listen. Selective listening is often not enough, as truly attentive listening is required. In sum, empathy involves both intent to be respectful and care (which is very different to sympathy) and action, which demonstrates such capacity and applies equally to familial and professional contexts (Dolan 2006; Lefevre 2010; Winter 2011).

SAM provides a useful tool to help counteract a lack of empathy in staff and promote a positive work culture, thus ensuring better relationship-based working with young people and families. It involves workers and management establishing and describing a set of work practice standards, ranging from induction processes such as confidentiality norms to assessment intervention and evaluation programme descriptors (Dolan 2006). Through the utilisation of self-service user and peer measurement, each worker sets enhancement goals (worked out through supervision). Through ongoing reflective practice, these self-goals are assessed over distinct time intervals with a view to enhanced working. The reflective practice process should not only apply at the individual worker or local manager level, but throughout organisations, as discussed in Chapter Three. Ultimately, reflective practice as a component of direct work with children, young people, families and communities, as well as peers, enables a process for self-checking a worker's quality of professionalism in service delivery. Utilisation of ongoing reflective processes affords the worker the opportunity to amend and enhance practices and to enhance the quality and effectiveness of professional relationships with others.

FAMILY SUPPORT PRINCIPLES AS TOOLS FOR DIRECT WORK

A core set of ten family support practice principles were set out in Chapter One earlier. These principles have been adopted in Irish child welfare services widely and utilised in the micro contexts of local service delivery (OMCYA 2007). In order to link the principles more closely to direct work in family support in Northern Ireland, local frontline staff under the guidance of senior management in child welfare services (McTiernan and colleagues) have integrated the ten principles into the Coram Star model. This enables practitioners to self-rate their compliance with each principle while placing the young person, parent and/or full family as the central focus point. In effect, this creates a set of reflective practice questions against which individual professionals and their managers can assess and explore how they are doing in relation to each or to all of the ten principles, with a view to either enhancement towards or retention of full compliance. This is graphically illustrated in Figure 4.4.

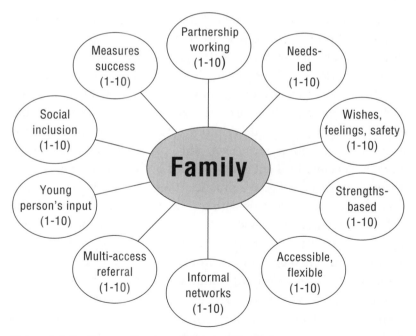

Figure 4.4: Scaling application of practice principles

CONCLUSION

This chapter has identified the key unifying components of direct work in family support, acknowledging that social support, resilience, social ecology and social capital, relationship and reflective practice are essential, underpinning theoretical concepts. While overviewing both licensed and localised programmes within the family support landscape, the point has been stressed that 'programmes don't make the worker'. The success of direct work is strongly connected to the capacity of workers to connect and kindle positive change for personal coping among those they work with, and do so with an explicit awareness that this occurs within a social ecology. Programmes of whatever type provide essential maps for practice, but without an engaged, authentic relationship, direct work will not succeed. Family support work is essentially about the capacity of one set of humans to engage with another. It is about engaging and expanding networks of support. Practitioners and their managers need to identify, engage, intervene and strengthen these through a supportive relationship that to be successful requires an authentic and trusting relationship in which *know of* (theory), *know how* (skill) and *know to* (reflective wisdom) are core and essential elements.

We propose the following reflective questions for service managers and practitioners to guide their practice:

1. How can I enhance service users' use of informal and natural sources of support, including extended family and community contacts? What are the practical steps required to lead to the enlistment of natural family support?

2. What are the best ways to ensure that my service spans non-stigmatising universal provision whilst also targeting work towards young people and families under stress?

3. How can I advance resilience promotion as a matter of routine practice in working with children, youth and families?

4. In the context of pressures in the delivery of established programmes, what practical steps can I take to ensure that my relationship with the person using the service is valued?

5. In what ways do I or my colleagues demonstrate active empathy towards the children, youth and families we work with and for?

6. Having a relationship of worth is a key factor in direct work in family support; how can I build connections with service users across the tasks of initial engagement, maintenance support and managing situations of personal crisis?

— Chapter Five —

FAMILY SUPPORT EVALUATION

INTRODUCTION

Running through this book is a desire to provide an account of family support and its various components and connected domains that is robust and that will serve as a benchmark on which thinking and critique can be based, and against which progress can be assessed in practice, policy and theory. Within any such assessment, evaluation plays a key role. In concrete terms, evaluation is the means by which the merit of family support approaches can be assessed. But evaluation studies can feed into the further development of thinking in family support, increasing knowledge in the underpinning theories, and in our understanding of policy, organisations and practices. In the absence of funding streams for exploratory research, evaluation research continues to be a significant basis for knowledge development in the field.

How, then, might the relationship between evaluation and family support be considered? One perspective is to see it as central to family support, as expressed in the ten principles set out in Chapter One. Thus, for something (policy, service, practice) to be family support, it has to incorporate a commitment to evaluation from the outset. In this way, a commitment to evaluation is part of the value base of family support. But evaluation is also separate from family support; it is a field of research, with its own broad rules, processes and methods. What happens when these are applied to family support? The argument that we make in this chapter is that family support evaluation is a specific type of activity, that is, the nature of family support and its core elements demand that evaluation should always incorporate a focus on a set of substantive concerns, and that certain orientations and methods should always feature in evaluation designs. We argue in this chapter in favour of the idea of 'developmental family support evaluation', that doing evaluation in family support builds from its theories and principles, and is a distinctive enterprise. Once again, the recognition of the openness of family support to draw from other fields and to be constantly in development is reflected in this chapter.

Evaluations in family support should include a focus on social support and social capital, on resilience and on the ecological nature of needs and solutions to them. Ideally, these will be as set out in the theory of change and/or logic model of an intervention, but in reality require 'unearthing' by an evaluator from the programme or project plans. The incorporation of a focus on its principles is a similar pre-requisite. Unlike the theories for family support, its principles are likely to be more readily present in the thinking of promoters of programmes and projects, and more easily understood as appropriate evaluation targets. Methodologically, we argue that an ideal family support evaluation has to be mixed methods in approach, incorporating participatory dimensions and attentive to reflective practice as a source of data. It should be driven by key concerns of not what works, but what works for whom in what circumstances, including when and where.

We build towards this position through this chapter, and begin by outlining the current context of a tension between approaches built on the idea of the experiment, and those favouring practice and the voice of those using services. The fundamentals of evaluation are then described, its relationship to family support illustrated through a set of examples, and a set of guiding questions offered for anybody embarking on evaluation in a family support context. Next, we outline the role of theory and specifically theories for family support (see Table 5.2 later). An interpretation of the meaning of process and outcomes in family support evaluation (concerns of most evaluations) is then provided. The final part of the chapter focuses on methodology and the overarching philosophical approach to knowledge development, before an integrative summary of the chapter's content and agenda for family support evaluation is presented.

CONTEXTS

One of the major questions for this century in policy circles is, what are the standards of evidence on which policy should be based (Dill and Shera 2012)? In general terms, the emergence of the evidence-based practice movement demonstrates the shift towards a view of intervention as only justifiable if its efficacy can be demonstrated using the highest standards of evidence, in which the 'gold standard' is the randomised control trial (RCT), an experimental method involving random allocation to control and intervention conditions. In the context of limited resources and significant competition for them among the various strands within social policy provision, in the UK, Northern Ireland and the Republic of Ireland, policy-makers have been attracted to the US, both in the search for 'what works', and for research and evaluation methodologies to establish this. Thus, a range of models of family support-relevant models of intervention (Multisystemic Therapy, Treatment Foster Care, Incredible Years, Big Brothers Big Sisters) have been adopted and adapted in these jurisdictions. Critically, alongside these 'best practice' models has been a methodological shift towards the social experiment.

Similarly, the emergence/re-emergence of experimental approaches has occurred alongside an increasing interest in and a reassertion of the significance of practice, and of the need for attention to the social space within which practitioner and service user interact. Best represented at a formal theoretical level in the area of reflective practice, as outlined in Chapter One, we propose it as the key 'theory for practice' of family support. The interesting question is, of course, reflective practice for what? If seen as a buttress to professional power, claims making, expertise development or self-interest, it is unlikely to find any hearing at policy level. For us, an important dimension of reflective practice within a family support context is its relevance to improving the lives of outcomes for the children and families served.

Balancing these strands have been significant developments in the relationship between the state and those using the services it provides or funds. In essence, the current era is one wherein, in various settings, those using services are more aware of their right to quality provision and are more likely to have access to structures and processes through which they can make their views known. In part, these developments reflect the consumerism theme, inherent in New Right values and carried forward in more recent New Labour/middle-way thinking. They are also an expression of key themes of empowerment, reflected, for example, in community development theories and values, and especially strongly in the approaches adopted within the disability sector (Leece 2004). Translated into the arenas of research and evaluation, the demand by various socially excluded groups is that, at a minimum, research does not treat them as objects and, more fundamentally, that they should have control of the full research agenda in terms of what should be researched, how and by whom. Thus, within the research and evaluation fields, specific methodologies and methods have been developed in line with these new demands, for example participatory action research (Kemmis, McTaggart and Nixon 2014) and empowerment evaluation (Fetterman 2001).

UNDERSTANDING EVALUATION

Before engaging more specifically in the demands of a specifically family support approach to evaluation, it is necessary to set out some general parameters on evaluation. While it is impossible to reflect the breadth and depth of the field in a single chapter, Table 5.1 sets out a framework reflecting core considerations in thinking about evaluation which are pertinent to family support. The first set concerns the intervention itself – plainly, evaluation choices are predicated on the nature of the intervention. Thus, the family support policy and service domain in which the intervention operates, its scale and its complexity are key factors in dictating the nature of evaluation. Similarly, what different stakeholders in interventions desire from evaluation is key – historically, this would have been a more narrow concern with funders' desires. While it is important not to overstate shifts in power, reflecting developments in evaluation theory and practice and in society and policy generally, what other stakeholders want, and especially service users, has become more important.

Table 5.1: A typology of approaches to family support evaluation

Criterion	Dimensions	Examples
Intervention domain	The policy area of the intervention/the dimension of children and young people's lives on which the intervention is focused	Study in community setting of project aimed at crime prevention, using youth diversion model School-based reading programme aimed at improving reading age
Scale of intervention	Scale as indicated by budget, staffing, reach, etc.	Major intervention on health visiting across city with 500 participating mothers Parenting programme delivered within a family support programme with 30 participating parents
Intervention complexity	The degree to which the intervention involves a single activity/limited set of common activities or a wider set of disparate but connected activities	Two-stranded programme incorporating intensive counselling with the young person and activity-based group work towards anger management Complex community initiative focusing on quality early development, comprising home visits to new parents, new curricula for pre-school providers, financial incentives for parents and a major publicity campaign focused on the importance of language development in young children

Cont.

Criterion	Dimensions	Examples
Intervention stakeholder requirements	What type of evaluation is required by the funder? What type of evaluation might be required to convince funder to support continued operation?	Evaluation focusing on accountability concerns – was the funding used as per initial proposals? Was the programme implemented as planned? Were there appropriate cost-controls? Evaluation focusing on early stage outcomes that indicate programme promise
Evaluation orientation	Two dimensions: *Formative/summative* Whether the evaluation is formative (concerned with assisting programme development) or summative (concerned with measuring the effects and impacts of the evaluation) *Process/outcome* Whether the evaluation is about the intervention processes (e.g., implementation-related questions on take-up, fidelity to models or plans) or about outcomes (whether the intervention succeeded in achieving the changes intended, for the child/young person, adult, population or service)	Formative evaluation of small-scale pilot programme aimed towards early identification and response of welfare needs of children in the community Summative evaluation focusing on key indicators of success of above programme, including, e.g., re-referral rates Process evaluation of a leadership-focused youthwork intervention examining take-up, satisfaction of participants with training programme and success or otherwise of delivery of model Outcome-focused evaluation focusing on changes in self-rated leadership capacity of young people and changes in levels of involvement in leadership work in the community

| Evaluation design/ methodological approach | The overall methodological approach to answering the evaluation questions. For example, options include: experimental, stakeholder, participatory, empowerment, utilisation-focused, theory-based | Quasi-experiment involving the delivery of a multistranded conflict management/violence prevention programme in community A, with pre- and post-measurement in community A and comparative community B

Evaluation of a community development initiative focused on developing representative community structures with explicit empowerment goals (e.g., leading/participating in the evaluation leads to community empowerment) |
|---|---|---|
| Evaluation methods | The type of research methods which the evaluation requires. These will fit under three broad headings: quantitative, qualitative, mixed | Evaluation of health promotion programme involving a battery of biological, psychological and attitudinal measures

Evaluation of a young mother's support programme built on focus group and individual interviews |

The second set of considerations emerges from thinking about evaluation as a set of practices. We can understand evaluation as involving different overall orientations, as formative or summative. Similarly, evaluation will involve overall methodological commitments, reflecting general orientations in social research towards quantitative, qualitative or mixed-methods approaches, or the myriad approaches within evaluation theory (from experimental to empowerment). Although ultimately the most significant in terms of their capacity to generate the data to arrive at judgements (a key imperative of evaluation research), method choices will stem from these orientations.

Flowing from this general framework, some of the key questions for anybody interested in doing evaluation in family support will be:

- In what domain does the intervention operate?

- What is the scale and complexity of the intervention?

- What are the requirements of the intervention's stakeholders?

- Is the evaluation orientation towards process or outcomes/impact, or both?

- What evaluation design most suits given answers to the foregoing questions?

- What methods accord with design choices?

Although much family support practice operates in small-scale contexts within limited funding, we argue that this does not preclude the possibility of evaluation – from the principles outlined, for something to be classified as family support, measurement/evaluation must be present. In the absence of funding, family support evaluation can be forwarded through ongoing self-evaluation and reflective practice.

THEORIES

Good practice is always underpinned by good theory, and it is safe to say that theories are embedded in all social interventions – either explicitly represented in theories of change or awaiting unearthing by an evaluator. What is less certain is how explicit and/or formalised theories are within programmes. In our view, family support evaluation requires a commitment to theories for two reasons. First, doing so enhances the validity and explanatory power of evaluation findings and analysis, by linking them to wider bodies of knowledge. Second, and the corollary of this, in the context of cost constraints on social research generally, knowledge generated in and through evaluation can strengthen theory. Taking the key theories outlined in Chapter One (social support, social capital, resilience, social ecology), it is easy to imagine a set of theoretically based evaluation questions that could be incorporated into any evaluation, whatever the scale or orientation. Table 5.2 sets out some examples.

Table 5.2: Theories for family support in evaluation

Theories	Examples of theory-based evaluation questions
Social support theory	Is the type of support being offered matched to the needs of those using the services?
Social capital theory	What sorts of bridging capital are apparent?
Resilience theory	Does the child have one reliable alliance?
Ecological theory	How do the micro- and meso-systems interact?

Within interventions that are based on logic models or theory of change approaches, theories will be explicit. These will be theories that underpin particular actions or sub-programmes and overall programme theory, which offers the rationale for why particular sets of activities, drawing on particular resources, in particular contexts, might arrive at particular outcomes. Even if such theorising is not explicit and documented in interventions, good evaluation practice will involve its unearthing, framing and articulation through dialogue with programme stakeholders.

In theorising family support, we make practice – what practitioners do and how they do it – a central concern, and argue that the field of reflective practice offers a set of useful theories and models for doing and thinking about family support. Within an evaluation frame, reflective practice can have at least two functions. First, it can be a substantive area of concern for an evaluation – to what extent are reflective processes embedded within individual worker practices and overall intervention practices, and with what impact on overall implementation? Second, reflective practice can be the source of key data and analyses for an evaluation; for example, a set of documented practitioner reflections might demonstrate patterns within an overall programme that on aggregate represent a plausible explanation for particular service user outcomes. The place of practice in family support evaluation is discussed further below.

As highlighted in Chapter Three, an emergent, relevant field for family support evaluation is that of implementation science. Now with a journal devoted to it, the field is currently strongly connected to evidence-based practice and the study of its implementation. Thus, much of the published work concerns how to implement programmes whose efficacy has been demonstrated by experimental studies or meta-analyses. Although limited somewhat by this overall orientation, the theorising and testing of implementation activity should lead to knowledge for practice in family support, and offer concepts and frameworks for evaluating programme implementation. For example, Fixsen *et al.* (2009) and Aarons *et al.* (2014) have developed encompassing models to support successful implementation, which are useful for studying the implementation of large-scale, innovative family support interventions. In these types of implementation science models, significant attention is paid to the characteristics of the organisation or service, the orientation of staff towards adopting new ideas, the environments in which the service operates, the specific nature of the intervention and the role of those who developed the intervention.

PROCESS

In general terms, process evaluations tend to focus on the 'hows' of interventions, answering the following kinds of questions:

- Is the programme reaching its intended target group?

- Are programme activities being delivered with fidelity to the programme model or plan?

- Are programme activities well organised?

- What factors in the implementation of the programme have contributed to programme success/failure?

Multiple, specific questions flow from these general questions, the volume of which will vary in relation to the scale and complexity of an intervention. For example, a large-scale parenting programme will require a detailed focus on how a programme is marketed generally, the specific approaches adopted to reach more disadvantaged parents, and the underpinning organisational structures and processes put in place to ensure that programme targets are met. Space doesn't allow for a full account of the theoretical bases of process studies here, but interested readers are directed to work by Patton (2008) and Rossi, Lipsey and Freeman (2004). One clear and accessible basis for process evaluation questions in family support exists in the set of practice principles, as outlined in Chapter Four. In Northern Ireland, the principles have been adapted for use by locality-based family support hubs, which aim to provide early intervention to children and families. They are encouraged to self-rate on the extent to which the principles are achieved, for example on being needs-led or on being strengths-based.

Practice

Evaluation theorist Schwandt (2005) provides a significant account which privileges practice in evaluation. He draws our attention to the importance of practice and the need for evaluation to attend to the "'rough ground" where values, personalities, evidence, information, feelings, sensitivities, emotions, affect, ambiguities, contradictions, inconsistencies, and so forth are simultaneously in play as we try to do the right thing and do it well' (p.99). Rather than seeing practice as what needs repair in order to deliver evidence-based social services, he argues that it is the key context within which changes occur for people. In this view, practice is not an object or phenomenon, but a social event, and therefore dynamic and dependent on and imbued with language and meaning. It is complicated – practitioners are neither totally autonomous and free to pursue their own interests, and nor are they 'dopes' carrying out roles in unreflective ways. Practice change involves more than increasing one's capacity to know 'that' or know 'how' – the fundamental changes in practice depend on the practitioner's change in their 'way of being' towards a situation. Knowledge doesn't exist separate to practice. Practice viewed thus requires evaluation to have the following commitments:

- There is an imperative at the heart of the actions of practitioners to evaluate, but this may be submerged or hidden from them, resulting in unreflective and uncritical approaches.

- It must be pedagogical – its processes must encourage evaluative thinking among practitioners.

- Deliberation about value is social and therefore dialogue-based.

- It must be orientated towards social justice concerns.

Within family support evaluation, practice requires significant attention.

OUTCOMES

The major shift in recent years within policy and services for children and families has been the elevation of outcomes to the position of a dominant paradigm. While there are many definitions of what exactly an outcome is, the general point is that services should be developed, implemented and evaluated driven by a focus on a set of desired statuses or changes in individual children and/or their parents, and possibly in services. The implication is that, in the past, the concern was more with what services did (outputs) than with what they achieved (outcomes) (Politt and Bouckaert 2004). In the UK, Northern Ireland and the Republic of Ireland, high-level policy statements have been developed that refer to the outcomes that the state seeks for its children (Chief Secretary to the Treasury 2003; Office of the First Minister and Deputy First Minister 2006; OMCYA 2007). Table 5.3 contains examples of outcomes that might be associated with family support programmes.

Table 5.3: Some outcomes

Improved pro-social behaviour/reduced anti-social behaviour	Reduced incidence of bullying
Improved relationships between children and parents	Increased self-care skills in the face of bullying
Increased parenting capacity (self-report capacity to effectively manage child's behaviour)	Increased knowledge of safe sexual health practices
Increased rate of school attendance	Reduced unsafe sexual health practices
Reduced rates of school expulsion	Increased levels of participation in out-of-school physical or mental health supporting activities
Literacy levels in line with population norm	Increased involvement in civic action
Reduction in numbers of children in care (and increase in children being cared for at home safely)	Increased political knowledge
Parents better able to cope	Increased involvement in advocacy actions (campaigning)
Enhanced support networks for parents	Reduced age for first sexual activity
Increased capacity to access support	Reduced age for usage of drugs including alcohol
Children ready for engagement with school/learning	Reduced self-report criminal/anti-social acts
Increased resilience (measured through increases in protective factors in child's life/reduction in risk factors)	Reduced arrests/cautions

This is not to say that the idea of all policy and service development being predicated on an outcomes focus is not contested. Indeed, various academics and researchers have critiqued outcomes and related market-driven approaches to policy development (Beresford 2005; Jones 2015; Krohn 2015). There is little doubt, however, that the emergence of an outcomes focus reflects more than New Right social policy. We can say that the emergence of outcomes reflects developments in and pressures from social science, social administration, service management and practice and user groups (Thompson 2008).

A starting assumption about family support evaluation is that *it matters* that services make a difference to the lives of those they are supposed to work with/for. One would expect that anybody working in services would accept this assumption. Similarly, it is reasonable to expect that a child, young person or parent accessing a service will hope that, at some level, the service will help them in some way, bringing about a change from a current unsatisfactory situation to one that they are happier with. In this sense, the result, impact, consequence or outcome of service delivery is of concern to people who receive and provide services. The literature on evaluation is replete with different approaches to conceptualising and defining outcomes, and with a variety of accounts of the connection with related concepts, for example needs and rights (Bouckaert and van Dooran 2003; Friedman, Garnett and Pinnock 2005; Hogan 2001). One straightforward approach to these connections is to make rights the highest level concept, and to see outcomes as a step on the way to meeting needs, which, if met, ensure that rights are achieved (Canavan 2010).

But the concept of outcome is problematic. One reason for this is that it has been appropriated by advocates of market-based solutions to social problems. In this approach, outcomes are essentially indicators of desirable social goods that have a price of provision (as reflected in the costs of policies or services). The value of the policy or service is its capacity to deliver outcomes. The core assumption is that the mechanism of the market that operates in the realm of individual consumption is the same as that required for the delivery of public goods that satisfies the needs of society (e.g., health, education, public safety, etc.). It is not necessary here to give examples of why market approaches are often inappropriate, can fail to deliver important public goods and why we need state intervention – again, echoing arguments developed in Chapter Two on policy choices. On the other hand, it is difficult to find a strong basis to reject the end point of market-based arguments – that services should result in the outcomes for which they are established. Indeed, the demand for services that achieve outcomes fits comfortably with theories that emphasise the rights of citizens, in the context of power imbalances with the state and its professional classes. The role of user movements in the disability sector in the UK provides a solid example, of the desire of people receiving services to have greater direct control in them – reflecting both a desire to influence what services do and what results they produce for people using them. An alternative vantage point from which to argue for attention to outcomes is to be found in individual, team and/or service motivation. Simply put, in order to function as a worker in social and education services, most people require an ongoing indication that they are achieving what they expect.

Another issue that arises in relation to outcomes is the ambition of the intervention. Given the level and multifaceted nature of difficulties faced by some children, young people and parents, it may be that an intervention or service can be characterised as effective, if they are seen to be coping in spite of various adversities. Coping as an outcome is one that will be relevant for family support interventions in the context of high levels of need and adversity – both on a short and long-term basis. Such considerations bring us towards wider questions on the nature of social problems and their provenance and solubility.

Thick outcomes

Our position in this book is that, on balance, outcomes will be a necessary focus in any evaluation, but there should be great caution in how they are approached. One way to incorporate a family support orientation into a consideration of outcomes is to ask who decided what the outcomes of the intervention were to be and how this was to be done. In doing so, this addresses process issues to do with participation by children and parents, a key family support principle. In terms of assessing outcomes, a key consideration is the role of the perspectives of parents and children.

Within current evaluation practice, data on perspectives has a low position on levels of evidence scales. Such a view can be supported through a simple example. Imagine a scenario where both children and parents express positive views about a service operating in a disadvantaged community, but as indicated by standardised and service-based measures, the children's situation has dis-improved radically in the areas targeted by the service, with no change in circumstances that might explain this. The service's efficacy would certainly be in question in such a scenario.

What does this imply for the meaning and value of the data on children's and parents' perspectives? One argument is that many parents will not feel able to be critical of services that they are receiving for free – they will feel indebted to those providing the services, and in an evaluation will not criticise. An additional dimension of this argument is that parents will fear losing a service, particularly without any promise of a different or better service. In such a scenario, a service is at least more likely not to receive a negative evaluation. The obvious criticism of this argument is that parents are presented as lacking knowledge (of their children's needs and their own rights) and, critically, power. If, however, parent evaluations are taken at face value, as reflecting those of people with knowledge and power, the data must be seen as valuable and requiring fuller interrogation vis-à-vis other sources. For example, services often have unintended outcomes or are used for different (although are still valuable to the child or parent) purposes than intended.

Currently, however, there is no strong guidance in the literature on how to combine different sorts of data on outcomes towards the aggregate statements of merit/value that are expected from evaluation research. Building from the interpretivist/ethnographic idea of understanding through thick description, one option is to develop sets of 'thick outcome' measures. Such measures would weight and combine a range of measures inclusive of service status, outcomes, standardised measures and children's, parents' and referrers' perspectives. Table 5.4 provides an example of a community-based paid mentoring service for children involved in both child protection and justice systems.

Table 5.4: Weighting of measures

Measure type	Specific measure	Weighting
Status measure	In community/in care	High
	Offences since intervention	
	In community/incarcerated	
	Involvement in supportive community networks	
Standardised measure	Strengths and Difficulties Questionnaire (Goodman 1997)	Medium
	Child Behavior Inventory (Eyberg and Pincus 1999)	
	Adapted Social Provisions Scale (SPS) (Dolan and Cutrona 2004)	
Attitudinal measure	Child's view on effect of service on behaviour	Low
	Parent's view on effect of service on behaviour	
	Referrer's view on effect of service on behaviour	
	Practitioner's view on effect of service on behaviour	

In this example, the key issue is whether the mentoring programme has been successful in keeping the young person in the community and increasing their involvement in wider positive networks and activities post-intervention. Standardised measures are indicative of changes in the young person's behaviour, while attitudinal measures reflect the perspective of various stakeholders on the intervention value. In a thick outcomes approach, the idea is to arrive at an overall rating, numeric or otherwise, which allows each source of outcome information to be included. The various sources could be accorded equal value in arriving at an overall rating, or they could be weighted as in the example, with one or more sources given more significance in the rating process. Thus, even if given a lower weighting, attitudinal measures are at least included as valid data in the assessment of change. Attention to these perspectives allows the possibility of discovering useful and not so useful aspects of intervention, while seeking a variety of views helps increase the validity of this type of data. Ideally, any stakeholders' ratings should be accompanied by qualitative examples that support the ratings.

METHODS

Our experience as family support researchers suggests that the start point in decisions about evaluation design and methods has to be the question or questions for which answers are being sought – methods follow questions. That said, ideas on appropriate methods evaluation are prefigured by the above sections on family support processes and outcomes. Thus, any evaluation in family support that doesn't seek to include the perspectives of stakeholders on processes and outcomes will at best be partial. Family support evaluation should include methods that at minimum access the voices of stakeholders, particularly children and parents, and at best do so in ways that equalise power relations among all stakeholders, including those between the evaluator and others. Generally, qualitative approaches will be more suited to accessing these sources of data. Yet, as outlined above, outcomes, and their quantification according to robust techniques, matter in family support – evaluation in family support also demands quantitative approaches. This leads to a view of family support evaluation requiring both – family support evaluation must be a mixed-methods endeavour.

While the idea of evaluations involving mixed methods is not new, there have recently been efforts to underpin the practice with stronger theory and definitions, most clearly represented in the establishment of the *Journal of Mixed Methods Research.* As Johnson, Onwuegbuzie and Turner (2007, p.6) indicate, the practical nature of evaluation research and the need for multiple sources of data in establishing the value of social programmes has meant that evaluators are more likely to have embraced mixed-methods research. Apart from the manifold theoretical and epistemological questions associated with mixed-methods thinking, the key practice question for an evaluator working within such a frame is, what is the relationship between the methods and the data they generate?

In practice, a mixed-methods design can be sequential or concurrent. In sequential designs, different methods are used at different stages. Thus, for example, a survey of parents participating in a parenting programme could be undertaken, allowing for generalisable findings on the value of the programme. Based on survey data, a qualitative study involving interviews could be developed, allowing for a deeper understanding of how the programme influenced parenting practices or not. In concurrent designs, qualitative and quantitative data is gathered at the same time, and either triangulated to help understand relationships between variables of interest, or nested, wherein one set of data is given more weight than another (Creswell *et al.* 2003). As Castro *et al.* (2010) highlight, methodological knowledge on how to integrate qualitative and quantitative data in practice is only now developing. Inasmuch as these are practical issues, they are also indicative of the tensions in the valuing of different types of methods and data by different social actors. On balance, policy-makers and funders are more likely to value quantitative accounts that allow generalisable findings that answer the 'does it work?' question, while other stakeholders may be more open. Our position is that family support evaluation should favour mixed methods in most cases.

BEING REALISTIC ABOUT FAMILY SUPPORT EVALUATION

While a detailed consideration of epistemology is not possible here, it is as important to our thinking about family support evaluation as our conceptual theories for family support set out in Chapter One. Thus, implicit in the arguments being made about the need to adopt a sophisticated stance on outcomes, to engage and understand the nature of practice and to recognise the need for mixed-methods approaches is an orientation to a realist epistemology of evaluation. Underpinning a realist approach are three major theoretical stances. First is a commitment to the idea that the world is real and not dependent on how we see or understand it. *There is a real social world*. Second, social science requires an open systems approach – in essence, social policies, programmes and services are affected by a range of influences, including macro-historical and institutional factors, and the choices and actions of individuals and groups (Katz and Pinkerton 2003b). Additionally, evaluation activities themselves are part of the context because they may affect what is being evaluated (Pawson 2006, p.18). For this reason, *context matters in evaluation*. Third, causality is seen as generative; it is not adequate for evaluators to simply discover whether intervention 'X' causes outcome 'Y'. It is necessary to understand the mechanisms, including the context, that are linked to the outcomes. Evaluators need to *identify the mechanisms that help explain why interventions work or don't work*. Because they are usually hidden, the major challenge for the realist evaluator is identifying the mechanisms (Astbury and Leeuw 2010). Taking these orientations together, the question, then, for realist evaluation is not 'what works?', but rather, 'what works, for whom, in what circumstances?', and in order to answer these questions, different methodologies and different types of data are required (Pawson 2006, p.25).

Kazi (2003) offers an example of realist evaluation in practice. Drawing on work with family centres in the UK, he outlines how practitioners were involved in selecting standardised measures for use in their work. These measures functioned as both tools for practice and as sources for evaluation processes. Drawing on these measures, in tandem with demographic, contextual and delivery data, Kazi demonstrates how realist evaluation can provide assessments on outcomes, and arrive at understandings of the mechanisms leading to them. Kazi, Pagkos and Milch (2011) highlight in particular the value of integrating realist approaches to family support evaluation with ongoing day-to-day management of and practice in services.

AN AGENDA FOR FAMILY SUPPORT EVALUATION

In offering a prescription for family support, perhaps the key start point is that it will be as 'messy' as the social world it should reflect. But in engaging in this fluid and sometime chaotic reality, we think that planning for and doing family support evaluation should involve consideration of at least some of the following questions:

1. Is it possible to use some or all of the ten family support principles as the basis for assessing programme implementation?

2. What role is theory playing in the evaluation? Does a theory of change guide the evaluation? What social and psychological theories underpin the intervention and the practices it comprises?

3. How is practice to be viewed within the evaluation? Can self-evaluation tools be incorporated? Does the evaluation involve meaningful dialogue with practitioners?

4. What kind of a mixed-methods approach is being adopted? What are the respective roles of quantitative and qualitative data? Which, if either, is privileged? Are they being implemented sequentially or in parallel?

5. What role do the ideas, viewpoints and accounts of children and parents play in the evaluation? Will they inform the evaluation design? Will parents and children have any governance or quality assurance role for the work? What approaches will be adopted to ensure meaningful participation?

6. How are outcomes understood in the evaluation? How are they to be measured? Are multiple approaches being adopted?

7. How is a focus on what works for whom in what circumstances going to be embedded in the evaluation design?

Most importantly, we suggest that these types of questions can be applied across all levels, from frontline practices to state policy. While more resources for evaluation should mean greater reliability, validity and more depth, these questions can direct even the smallest-scale family support efforts.

— *Chapter Six* —

CONCLUSION
FAMILY SUPPORT AS A GLOBALISING AGENDA

INTRODUCTION

In concluding this book, there is one further aspect of understanding and implementing family support that needs to be considered – the international dimension. This chapter argues for the importance of family support practitioners, whether they are policy-makers, managers, frontline staff or researchers, taking a global perspective when thinking about, developing and delivering family support. This will involve returning to the 'cupped model' of family support discussed in Chapter One (see Figure 1.2) in order to draw attention to the way that the global institutions and processes as part of the social ecology of family support underpin and help shape the national and local agenda. While it can be asserted that family support 'now occupies a significant place within the array of care and welfare interventions' and has 'a global currency' (Dolan *et al.* 2006, p.11), it needs to be recognised that work on articulating and understanding the implications of such statements is at a surprisingly early stage. With limited attempts at cross-national knowledge exchange and international studies (Daly *et al.* 2015; Hellinckx, Colton and Williams 1997; Katz and Pinkerton 2003a), a comparative, global perspective on family support is still a goal for the future. There is a pressing need to move beyond a passive recognition of globalisation as context in order to actively integrate an international perspective into reflective family support practice.

By exploring family support in other countries, practitioners gain a set of international reference points that can provide challenging new ways of thinking and fresh ideas about family support at national and local levels in their own countries. 'By exploring the space family support occupies in other countries reflective practitioners gain a better understanding of how to see what is possible in their own' (Millar 2006, p.98). These fresh perspectives from cross-national comparison can help to surface dimensions that tend to lie hidden as given assumptions in national debate – not least the configuration of structures of power (Smith 2008). Cross-country reference points can also map out international connections that express the globalising nature of family support. Not only can international thinking and exchange help shape the policy and practice space in individual countries, but it firmly attaches family support to the global agenda for children and their families advanced by the UNCRC. This has been recognised by the UN Children's Fund (UNICEF), one of the leading global institutions in the field of children and families:

> UNICEF places family support and parenting support at the core of its global social protection agenda. We at the Office of Research believe that a newly emerging global body of evidence will contribute to stronger policy, more efficient interventions and increased cross-country learning. In years to come we hope to see more emphasis on linking national and international family-related policy goals to positive results for children and adolescents. (Daly *et al.* 2015, Foreword)

Realising that hope requires conviction among family support practitioners, whether they are policy-makers, managers, frontline staff or researchers, that their concerns are part of a global field of endeavour, they will also need to have confidence in their capacity to reflect on their work through a global lens. An international perspective has, and will increasingly have, a challenging role to play in teasing out and addressing key issues for each of the five areas of family support covered in the previous chapters: policy and politics; organisation, management and planning; development of practice models and programmes; direct work with children, families and communities; and research and evaluation. In response to the challenge of how to proactively engage with the global dimension of family support, this chapter aims to clarify why this is such an important area for reflective practice, to explore how to go about it, and to make some suggestions as to what reflective questions require early attention in order to internationalise each of the five other areas of family support covered in previous chapters.

THINKING GLOBALLY ABOUT FAMILY SUPPORT

In the late 1990s the UN Development Programme identified four structural changes that it anticipated would have an impact on human institutions across the world as it entered a new millennium: new global markets (e.g., deregulated financial services); new global actors (e.g., international NGOs); new rules and norms (e.g., human rights conventions); and new modes of communication (e.g., the internet and mobile phones) (cited in Payne and Askeland 2008). Those changes have occurred, and have created through their interaction a dynamic force for macro-level economic, political and cultural global change (B. Axford 2013; Sassen 2007). That dynamic contains within it opportunities for progressing global wellbeing through the exchange of knowledge and advanced technologies and a growing sense of mutual global social and political responsibility. The same global dynamic, however, can also undermine social development and social justice through creating economic, social and political instability, chosen and forced migration and the spread of disease (Lyons, Manion and Carlsen 2006; Palattiyil, Sidhva and Chakrabarti 2016; Williams and Graham 2014). The costs and benefits of globalisation are not evenly distributed but follow and compound the economic, social and geographical fault lines of local, national and international inequality. Individual experiences are interlocked with processes and institutions sited not just at the local but also the national and international levels – as poignantly captured by this comment on the impact of Structural Adjustment Programmes (SAPs) promoted by global institutions such as the International Monetary Fund and the World Bank:

SAPS do not exist merely as a policy or theoretical abstraction: it is people's lives that immediately become structurally adjusted in the process. When a government is ordered to cut back expenditure on health, education and welfare for example, it is *this* mother who cannot afford to send her child to school and it is *this* mother who cannot prevent her child from dying. (Sewpaul 2004, p.37; emphasis in original)

Thus in one sense the reason for needing to develop an international perspective on family support is strikingly obvious – globalisation. While family in its increasingly varied forms continues to have a core function in meeting social care needs everywhere in the world, it is equally clear that, as a social institution, the family is everywhere undergoing change, and in its various contemporary forms and functions is under immense pressure (Finn, Nybell and Shook 2010; Mills 2014). The reasons for this are both shared and varied internationally – shifting demographics, distribution of employment, forced migration through political violence, the spread of HIV/AIDS and changing expectations around age and gender roles, to name but a few. Along with the boundaries of nation-states, family support policy and practices within them are being challenged by cross-national economics, politics and culture. The growth of global health and welfare markets driven by the logic of neo-liberal economics has lowered social rights and labour standards, and increased reliance on private provision and informal support (Yeates 2014).

Globalisation is about time and place (B. Axford 2013; Sassen 2007). Events happening in one part of the world rapidly produce global effects, as dramatically shown by the international financial crisis of 2007–08 and the European refugee crisis of 2015. Globalisation enables and stimulates an increasing number and quickening speed of movement of people from country to country for a wide variety of reasons – as a leisure pursuit, looking for work, advancing careers and hoping for personal safety (Williams and Graham 2014). Information technology enables flows of capital, goods and services, prompting global integration of national business activities and economies. It links the deepening of networks of economic, social and cultural exchange that routinely transcend national borders with an ever quickening pace of those interconnections. Ever more porous national boundaries are also open to all sorts of cross-national social and cultural influences. Flows of images, ideas, information and values through media and communications worldwide spread a range of ideologies – not only the consumerism and possessive individualism of the 'American dream', but also the asceticism and collectivism of 'jihadist Islam'. All these developments stimulate international political movements and political action, set the challenge of political cooperation between nation-states and promote recognition of the need for overarching global political institutions.

All of globalisation's characteristics impact on family life. This is manifest in particular ways in different countries and in different cultural contexts (Chambers 2012; Mills 2014; Wells 2009), but key themes are apparent (Katz and Pinkerton 2003b):

- increasing diversity, fragmentation and uncertainty within family life and the community

- shifting and technologically transformed communication and support systems between parents and children and among extended family, friends and neighbours

- changing expectations of family relationships and the balance of power between men, women and children, including recognition of the importance of active fathering

- increasing behavioural, emotional and social problems for children and young people seen in delinquency, mental health and early parenthood.

While globalisation may be the obvious driver for taking an international perspective on family support, it is also important to be mindful of the contested and complex nature of the concept. There continue to be considerable differences as to how the phenomenon is understood and regarded (Yeates 2014). There is no consensus as to exactly what implications it has for understanding the past, making sense of the present, or charting the future. Part of the problem is the intellectual challenge of capturing within a unifying perspective the complex range of phenomena that globalisation is trying to address. Not only is it trying to encompass economic, demographic, cultural, social, political and psychological international trends, but trying to do so while many aspects of these phenomena themselves remain imprecisely described and understood at national and local levels. In addition, there are deep value-based political divisions over whether globalisation promotes or impedes human wellbeing (Midgley 2004).

Early studies of globalisation emphasised convergence and the flattening of local and national cultures and the hollowing out of nation-states. More emphasis is now placed on how these cultures and systems are 'remade' by global forces, with distinctive national features being retained alongside increasing international convergence and cooperation. Along with the sense of opening possibilities that goes with globalisation, as stressed by its supporters, there is an ever increasing sense of insecurity, stressed by those who oppose it. The speed and openness to change is closely associated with an increased sense of volatility and risk. This twin impact of globalisation is felt by all family members, but is especially pertinent to those who have a high degree of dependence – particularly children and young people (Chambers 2012; Finn *et al.* 2010; Mills 2014):

> The complexity, pressures and change which characterise contemporary family life reflect not only shifting cultural expectations about personal relationships but also changing patterns of work, housing, transport and leisure within the context of national and global socio-economic structures of inequality. Changes in the structure and context of family life had coincided and contributed to moral uncertainty surrounding the institution. (Pinkerton and Katz 2003, p.10)

The pressure and pace of change that globalisation places on the capacity of families to cope with social care needs has major implications for the form and function of state services. Changing patterns of family life and the associated implications for providing social care driven by globalisation is prompting many governments to review the form and function of state welfare provision (Welbourne and Dixon 2013). In pursuit of advantage in the global market, terms such as the 'investment state', 'developmental state' and even 'competition state' have been gaining in influence (Patel 2005; Spratt 2009; Stafford *et al.* 2012). States are also mindful of their obligations under the UNCRC, as the most advanced and overarching expression of a global agenda for children and young people within their families.

In the Preamble to the UNCRC, the importance of family life and obligation to provide family support is explicitly stated:

> The family, as the fundamental group of society and the natural environment for the growth and well being of all its members and particularly children, should be afforded the necessary protection and assistance so that it can fully assume its responsibilities within the community. (UN 1989)

The UNCRC provides an essential framework for thinking about the various rights, needs, informal supports, formal services and mandated interventions to be found in different countries. It covers all aspects of a child's life, setting out the civil, political, economic, social and cultural rights that all children everywhere are entitled to. Its articles underpin many of the goals and agreements established by the UN, and provide a mandate to many of the policies and activities of UN agencies, funds and programmes. It also sets out how adults, particularly parents, and governments must work together to make sure that children can enjoy all their rights. It provides benchmarks through its 54 articles to consider the quality not only of children's lives, but also of family life. By establishing a global framework it allows for cross-country comparison and helps to identify what is emerging as the key themes of convergence and divergence internationally.

In ratifying the Convention, state parties commit to supporting not just children and young people, but also their families. This is stated in a number of ways through various articles. Article 9 states that only in exceptional cases, such as evidence of abuse or neglect, should both parents not care for their children. Article 10 asserts that families living apart should be facilitated to maintain contact. Article 18 maintains that parents are the most important people in the lives of their children and should be supported by the state to fulfil this role. Article 27 gives children the right to a standard of living that is good enough to meet their physical and mental needs and places a responsibility on governments to help families achieve this.

In pursuit of children's rights and in response to the types of global pressure on family life noted above, services are being developed which, although expressed in particular ways in different countries, appear to share a range of characteristics, suggesting an emerging common direction of travel:

- Broad agreement on desired outcomes: prevention of child maltreatment and family breakdown; more effective parenting; improved family functioning; and improved educational, social and emotional functioning.

- Mixed economy of provision driven by a market logic in which even public services should be regarded as being delivered to 'customer citizens', emulating private service sector provision to its customers.

- Services need to show they are effective and cost-effective – market testing the most effective means to achieve this.

- Emphasis on targeting and therefore elevated importance of assessment.

While there may be a general momentum for change in a particular direction, that direction is still contested. It is also not articulated in a uniform fashion, directed by a coherent set of aims and objectives, rooted in a code of common values and informed by a shared theoretical perspective. Any attempt to survey existing family support will quickly show different state and cultural/economic contexts. These lead to different strategic priorities in regard to policy frameworks, types of service, forms of service delivery, target populations and relevant programmes (Daly *et al.* 2015). At the same time it is also apparent that states are concerned to learn from international experience: 'In their quest for new ideas policy actors increasingly look to how other states have managed similar problems and what lessons there are to learn from those experiences' (Millar 2006, p.88).

As noted in Chapter Four, this has led to some programmes and approaches gaining a global status, such as Family Group Conferences, Signs of Safety and Triple P-Positive Parenting. In the main, however, globalisation of family support is expressed in a more general recognition of the need for a series of shifts in emphasis: away from fragmented responses to expressed need, towards strategic responses to assessed need; from well-meaning, intuitively responsive programmes to evidence-informed service design; and from locally developed to nationally driven policy and practice. Addressing these shifts requires adoption of ecological models as the basis for understanding needs and services and developing theories of change. At the same time as this broadening of perspective, there is also a narrowing of focus, with the requirement to show that policy and programmes are working to achieve in a cost-effective manner the objectives of the policy-makers, practitioners and service users. Many of these developments can be framed as the imposition of neo-liberal economics and politics on family support, and yet there is also an emerging commitment to an empowering, preventative and rights-based value base.

Given the cross-currents within family support internationally, suggesting elements of both convergence and divergence, and consensus and contest, the field is best seen as expressing a range of shared dilemmas:

Promotion of out-of-family day care to facilitate flexible working in pursuit of increased productivity

VERSUS

Pressure on parents to demonstrate their competence as carers and spend 'quality time' with their children, tailoring services to meet local need and to show cultural sensitivity

VERSUS

Internationally validated evidence-based provision implemented
with high-fidelity. Centralised, joined-up strategies,
ensuring standardised quality and equality of access

VERSUS

Decentralised, flexible, local and, if required, rapid service
response. Increasing competence through professionalisation

VERSUS

Democratising provision through adult and child
service user and community involvement.

It is clear from both the tentative state of the international field of
family support and the challenge of the dilemmas that are apparent
that there is an urgent need for further elaboration, debate,
adaptation and refinement of the concepts, processes and practices
that express family support as a global theory, policy and practice.
Faced with this challenge, family support practitioners need to
reflect on how globalisation is impacting on the needs they are
grappling with, and consider how other countries are tackling the
same or similar issues, or if not, why not. This requires recognition
of globalisation as shaping the agenda of contemporary family
support. International comparison provides a means to trace
patterns of convergence and divergence, and to open the way to
considering what lies behind these patterns, thereby sharpening the
focus on what constitutes the essential features of family support:

> In extending the [Sheffield Children's Centre's] service provision
> principles internationally, the centre workers drew from the same
> philosophical well-spring as that which had driven their UK-based
> work...the decision to work abroad [Ethiopia, Jordan, Pakistan,
> Zimbabwe, Ireland] emerged as naturally from the centre's day-
> to-day activities as had other aspects of service development...
> responding, as before, to perceived need in communities with
> whom they already identified for a wide range of reasons and

in whom they recognised a marginalised status that could be improved with affirmative action. (Broadhead *et al.* 2008, p.79)

HOW TO THINK GLOBALLY ABOUT FAMILY SUPPORT

Despite the urgency and importance of the challenge, the previous section should have made it clear that a tentative approach to viewing family support through the lens of globalisation and international comparison is advisable because of the very real difficulties there are in undertaking such work. Theoretically it requires multilevel and multidimensional modelling that takes account of both shifts in place and time in order to 'unpack the spaces it [family support] occupies at both policy and practice levels in particular periods' (Featherstone, cited in Millar 2006, p.89). This involves a complex and demanding process of knowledge management, requiring both data collection and analytical skills. The UNICEF Innocenti Research Centre's project 'Family and parenting support: policies, practice and outcomes' is a useful illustration of these challenges.[1] It starts with the assumption, in line with the argument of the previous section, that family support is already an important part of national social policies and social investment packages. It usefully nuances this by pointing out that it applies primarily to high-income countries, while noting that there is an increasing interest in family support programmes in lower and middle-income countries.

The aims of UNICEF's project are to contribute to the global evidence that can guide the development of family-oriented policies and programmes in different contexts, and to showcase the best evidenced practice models. It is concerned with a broad range of multidimensional outcomes for children and adolescents – early childhood development, adolescent wellbeing, prevention of violence and family separation, and reduction of inequality. Designed to run for three years (2014–17), the first phase of the project reviewed existing policies, models and understandings of family and parenting support. This was in order to develop a

---

1   See www.unicef-irc.org/research/263

conceptual and analytical framework rooted in the experience of countries from both the Global North and Global South (Daly *et al.* 2015). The second phase focuses on existing programmes in order to develop theories and mechanisms of change applicable to low-income settings. In a final third stage, promising approaches will be tested in selected low-income settings to determine social and structural influences and the relationship between policy, intervention, context, mechanism and outcome:

> We believe that the lessons from Chile, Jamaica, the Philippines and South Africa are equally insightful as those from high income countries such as England and Sweden. The global perspective allows us to see not only the role of national governments but also that of regional bodies and international agencies, as key players in promoting child well-being through supporting parents and families. (Daly *et al.* 2015, Foreword)

This attention to both the Global North and Global South, with particular attention to low-income countries, is not only a response to the extent of need – economic underdevelopment, rapid urbanisation, dislocation of access to extended family, limited education and health provision, political instability – but is also recognition that all too often what passes for international exchange is actually the export of minority world experience, including copyrighted intellectual products, to the majority world. There is insufficient attention to fit between learning from the Global North and the realities of the Global South and no consideration to what the North could learn from the experience and practices of the South. Both the developed and developing world have much to learn from each other about the various forms and intermeshing of formal and informal supports for family life:

> Policy transfer does not involve the wholesale 'copying and pasting' of legislation, policy and practice from one country to another but rather 'lesson learning' and adapting policy and practice to correspond with cultural, institutional, and administrative arrangements. (Millar 2006, p.89)

Indeed, as the process of international exchange is better understood, it seems likely that even moving from thinking about 'implementation gap' to 'goodness of fit' is insufficient. To capture the lived, multidimensional and multilevelled reality will require 'a move from "policy transfer" to "policy translation"…a shift in "register" or "vocabulary" to explore more fluid, dynamic and messy processes' (Clarke *et al.* 2015, p.16).

That said, however provisional, some definition of family support is necessary as a starting point for a global conversation. Interestingly, UNICEF's project, at least in its first stage, made a distinction between 'family support' and 'parenting support', regarding them as having distinct orientations. However, in discussing this distinction, it is apparent that parenting support can actually be subsumed into family support:

> Parenting support is the narrower of the two, being focused on parents and parental engagement and practices. It is therefore not necessarily oriented to the unit of the family or to wider familial considerations. Family support is broader, concerned with the family as a social unit and its ecological balance – the relationships and resource flows between members as well as how well the family is embedded within supportive networks. Hence, family support is oriented to family stability and general family functioning as against the more parent-centred objectives of parenting support. (Daly *et al.* 2015, Foreword)

The crucial theoretical and practical point is that understanding family support requires attention to the social ecology of family life, involving informal support networks as well as formal support services. This social ecology of family support (see Figure 1.1 in Chapter One) includes the global level – both cross-national and international processes and institutions. To understand the dynamics of this social ecology it is necessary to go beyond a 'weak' ecology of nested levels in which the macro-international plate provides the foundational shape that in turn shapes the national, local and family levels above it. A 'strong' version of ecological modelling is more useful. It stresses that the dynamic interactions between the different levels not only shape the characteristics of the levels themselves, but are also the source of a 'dynamics of development in which outcomes are always contingent and transitory and every outcome is also an input' (Katz and Pinkerton 2003b, p.321).

This strong version of ecological modelling can usefully be characterised as an 'open systems perspective', in which process and outcomes are never entirely controllable or predictable. This transactional model of development is concerned to identify how change is driven by the constantly shifting balance of power within economic forces, political priorities, demographic pressures and organisational capacity. While conflict is seen as potentially disruptive and wasteful, it is also seen as potentially creative and dynamic. The aim of critical reflection is to understand the restrictions and opportunities for action emerging and dispersing within an actor's field of influence. So, for example, a family centre manager struggling to retain a welfare rights service in the face of local authority cutbacks may find a way to retain the onsite expertise of the advice worker through incorporating benefits advice as an aspect of services to refugee families for which there is new central government funding as part of a European Union (EU) crisis response.

This open systems theory of change can be schematically captured in a horizontal logic model of family support (see Figure 6.1). It is focused at the level of a particular family and a specific family support intervention. At the same time, it makes clear that any family intervention will impact on and be influenced by the local social ecology of formal and informal support that the family draws on to boost its social capital and resilience. As noted in the cupped model discussed in Chapter One (see Figure 1.2), this local social ecology not only includes extended family and friends, school and neighbourhood, community, voluntary and statutory organisations, but is also influenced by national and international systems. A family support intervention will not only be part of the local level, but will also be situated within organisational and policy systems that will, in turn, be part of interlocking national and international systems. In many countries there will also be a number of administrative and political levels between the local and the national, such as the Scottish, Welsh and Northern Ireland Assemblies in the UK. There are also regional cross-national structures between the national and the international that may need to be taken into account, such as the EU.

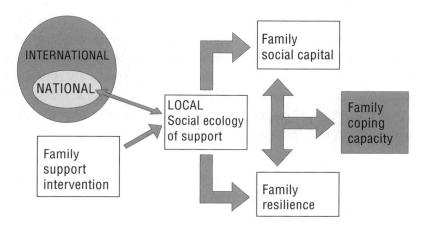

Figure 6.1: A global social ecology of family support

Recognition of these layers of influence brings with it the challenge of not only knowing and working with a local social ecology of support, drawing together formal and informal social support, but also being able to describe and relate proactively with the other layers. An open systems perspective assumes these will be ever shifting layers of organisational structures, policy and legislation, running from the local through the national to the regional cross-national and the international. Such is the nature of contemporary, globalised welfare provision (Daly 2011; Stafford *et al.* 2012; Yeates 2015). As the family centre illustration above and the detailed account of the Sheffield Children's Centre's international activities (see Broadhead *et al.* 2008) suggest, such fluid open systems hold out opportunities as well as restrictions.

Gathering the necessary information to describe and analyse the local and national components and dynamics of a social ecology is a daunting enough task. Adding a cross-national and global dimension to that may seem overwhelming. Undoubtedly the huge amount of information ever more easily accessed through the internet helps – although it is important not to underestimate the extent of the continuing 'digital divide', both in terms of who can access that material and who can add to it. In addition, many people, particularly those with English as a first language, continue to be limited to only one language. Translation can also be an issue in terms of making sense of information coming from the social, economic and political contexts of family life and family support services in another country, and in terms of how family support services to families are organised. And while information may be accessible, it may not be reliable or comparable across jurisdictions.

It is worth recalling a cautionary note struck over 20 years ago about engaging with international comparison:

> It is increasingly acknowledged that developments in any single country cannot be explained without setting them in the context of wider – global – changes. Yet there is a danger that the new orthodoxy may make it rather easy to espouse a comparative approach without being quite clear why or what questions can be most helpfully illuminated through comparison. (Cochrane 1993, p.1)

While there will be a global dimension to all family support interventions, the first step to explicitly engaging with it must be to clarify the particular purpose of the engagement. This may appear easier to do for a researcher in UNICEF than a family centre manager in a local community, but it is a challenge for both. The answer will lie in the work they are already engaged in – UNICEF's dissemination of best practice from around the world; the family centre manager's welfare rights service. UNICEF needs to understand how different models of family-related services have evolved in different parts of the world. The family centre manager needs to understand how an existing approach to welfare rights may need to be modified to meet the needs of refugees coming from a particular part of the world.

There are also a number of general approaches that help when thinking about internationalising family support work. Three approaches that have been identified are, to paraphrase the original, the 'global', the 'comparative' and the 'open exchange' (Payne 2006, pp.179–180). The first pursues an all-encompassing framework.

It assumes that it is possible to understand globalisation and the associated global processes and phenomena as a single system by using a number of key ideas within a single unifying theoretical framework. These ideas provide the conceptual currency for global understanding and international exchange. In the field of family support, globalisation as a variant of social ecology theory might provide the theoretical framework and encompass key concepts such as family, social support, social capital and resilience. This approach is clearly not easy. It requires complex data identification, management and analysis to meaningfully link local, national and international material together through the use of global concepts. There is also an absence of theoretical agreement about what the key concepts in the field of family support should be, and how they configure in intervention logic modelling.

The comparative approach sets out to better understand a particular phenomenon, such as family support, which is thought to exist in a number of national contexts, by 'confronting the differences between them, rather than asserting their wholeness' (Payne 2006, p.179). From this perspective, globalisation means understanding convergences and divergences in how the needs of families are understood and in how they might be met in different ways. In addition to comparing and contrasting national experiences against each other, global standards, such as those provided by the UNCRC, can be used to direct information collection and to benchmark countries. Given that Article 181 of the Convention requires state parties to 'render appropriate assistance to parents and legal guardians in the performance of their child-rearing responsibilities', the regular reports that countries are obliged to make to the UN committee on the Rights of the Child provide a good starting place for information on what assistance is being provided.

The open exchange approach is much less overtly instrumental than the other two. 'In this approach, we do not seek wholeness through one perspective. Instead, we value the discourse between perspectives as constructing a whole while exploring and valuing difference' (Payne 2006, p.180). This requires a much looser, although no less information-rich, exploration through dialogue around the various perspectives on an issue that exists in different countries. The aim is to provide a mutually enhanced understanding of the meanings that surround an issue in a way that generally promotes a global sensibility. This enriched perspective will help those engaged in the dialogue with the critical review and creative development of their own services in ways that make sense to them, irrespective of what others may take from the exchange. Such exchanges can be expected to reveal as much about the differing assumptions that underlie national cultures, politics and economics as about the needs and services particular to family support. For example, discussion of whether the children's rights base to family support is weakened in the US by the country not being a signatory of the UNCRC is just as likely to lead to discussion of the role of lobbyists, philanthropy and the relations between state and federal structures as to the politics of international affairs and UN agencies.

Which approach is adopted will reflect what is of interest to those directly involved in it, and what the purpose is of any particular internationalising activity. It also has to reflect what is feasible given existing resources – resources both in terms of the formal family support systems that exist within different countries and the resources that are available to undertake comparative work. The approach taken by UNICEF's 'Family and parenting support' project involved commissioned researchers, staff in UNICEF country and regional offices, and consultations with national and international experts. For the family centre manager, web searches and perhaps a Skype call is likely to have to suffice. That said, the Sheffield Children's Centre's experience shows that more is possible. Work with local Irish, Pakistani, Ethiopian and Eritrean communities in South Yorkshire, contact with a Jordanian woman involved with pre-school play provision and a visit to the centre by a Zimbabwean AIDS campaigner all led to work with families undertaken on behalf of and within those countries (Broadhead et al. 2008). The account of the centre's workers' openness to the internationalised nature of what they do may be less unique than it appears, as insufficient effort has gone in to documenting and evaluating such initiatives.

Whatever the scale or level of the activity, national-level information for individual countries has to be sourced from relevant national laws, statutory guidance and regulations, government statistics and academic research. The global level requires information from and about international institutions, documents and processes (N. Axford 2013; Deacon 2007). Once cross-national comparison is undertaken, the question arises as to whether some sets of countries look more like each other than other sets. This is an important question for international comparison of family support in determining existing and possible future patterns of convergence and divergence. Considerable work has been done within social policy on sorting out countries according to a classification based on three basic types of welfare regime: conservative, liberal and social democrat (Powell and Barrientos 2011). The positioning of a country within one or other of these clusters is judged according to how dominant two characteristics are within its welfare provision. One of these is the extent of decommodification, which is reflected in whether services are provided as of right and make it possible to sustain a livelihood without participation in the market. The other is the degree to which the state reduces social stratification and promotes social solidarity. Social democratic welfare regimes score high on decommodification and social solidarity with the purpose of state support for the common good. Liberal welfare regimes have low levels of decommodification and high social stratification with the purpose of freeing the market and allowing individuals to optimise their potential. Conservative welfare regimes have medium levels of decommodification and social solidarity, and state provision is used to maintain traditional structures of power and authority, both between the state and civil society and within civil society.

This typology is helpful for comparison as it suggests hypotheses to focus the work. For example, from the description of the types of regime it might be predicted that liberal regimes will pay little attention to state services to bolster family support. Conservative regimes will be more concerned to ensure arrangements that promote the work of NGOs and faith-based organisations in shoring up the traditional family. By contrast, social democratic regimes will be prepared to provide extensive state family support to children and their carers, whatever the particular variation on family life is being adopted. It is worth stressing again that the purpose of the typology is not to squeeze complex national experiences into the three categories, but to provide a means of sorting through and reflecting on that complexity.

It is also important to note that the welfare regimes approach has limitations and is constantly being called into question. As noted earlier, it is important that thinking globally reflects the experience of both the Global South and Global North. It should not be restricted to the application of thinking based on the minority world experience. Even though countries outside of Europe have been categorised using the three-regime typology, it has been argued that this was done by incorporating them into the model's very European terms rather than giving real expression to their own national and regional characteristics. A further concern is that the categories reflect a binary productionist/dependency view of social protection that is focused on redistribution of cash benefits from those with employment to those without. This fails to incorporate the insights of a more holistic, gendered and child-centred social policy that reframes social care as a particular form of labour, generally female, a moral obligation and responsibility and 'an activity with costs, both financial and emotional, which extend across public/private boundaries' (Daly and Lewis 2000, p.285).

From the latter, more holistic social care perspective, the mutual benefits of the interdependence of material production and social reproduction come more clearly into focus. Questions are raised about the social care infrastructure in different countries, and the shifting balance between the family, community, state and market within it. This perspective also prompts questions about how those configurations are driven by power relations based on class, age, gender, race and disability that are constantly being contested (Smith 2008). These questions resonate well with what is now known about the central importance for family support of the processes and dynamics of interdependence, both within and between formal and informal social support networks (Featherstone 2006).

Driving forward work on global thinking about family support from its present, very formative stage requires more than just speculation and swapping information in a loosely managed fashion. It would benefit from a project around which those interested in better understanding and developing the internationalisation of family support could focus. UNICEF's project, with its aim of reframing social protection as family support, might serve that purpose well. With different degrees and forms of engagement, family support practitioners of whatever type – policy-makers, managers, frontline staff or researchers – could synchronise their particular internationalising activity by reference to UNICEF's project and the UNCRC. This could facilitate identifying different approaches taken within different countries, and whether these 'natural experiments' suggested that certain approaches get better results with certain groups in relation to particular goals within particular local social ecologies. It could also prompt critical questioning of the purpose of state engagement that lies behind the choice of particular approaches and their goals.

UNICEF's work already provides something of a global benchmark through summarising the trends suggested by the existing policy and research literature identified through a comprehensive web search, evidence gathered by UNICEF country and regional offices, and by consultation with experts in the field. It also presents case studies from nine countries – Belarus, Chile, China, Croatia, England, Jamaica, the Philippines, South Africa and Sweden. It has confirmed that concerns about the conditions and practices relating to children's wellbeing and development are leading to a growth in provision of family support. In some cases this has meant the introduction of new policies and provisions, and in others, it involved a re-orientation or reframing of existing policies. However, government engagement was uneven internationally and took a variety of forms. In some regions, for example in South-East Asia and sub-Saharan Africa, systematic, government-led support initiatives were found to be rare. Other regions where family support was developing strongly included Western Europe, Central and Eastern Europe, Latin America and a few countries in Africa and Asia.

An additional resource to be had from this project is the guidance on methodology and conceptualising family support. It presents a framework that can help generate information from diverse national experiences that would inform the 'global', the 'comparative' or the 'open exchange' approaches discussed above. UNICEF's guidance will be developed further in later stages when promising approaches are tested. In this way, just as important as the benchmarking overview provided by UNICEF's project is the agenda it sets for further work:

The research highlighted some key priority areas as being in need of further analysis or possibly a programme of research:

- identification and analysis of the policies and interventions that are being rolled out in the name of family and parenting support in a local context, and national and regional variations in this regard

- the implementation and operationalization of provision in practice; the principles and ways of working with children, adolescents, parents, families and communities that are being promoted; strengths and weaknesses of provision; and the resources being deployed for the purposes of family and parenting support (among other possible interventions)

- the distribution of interventions across age groups, and the specificities and needs in this regard, especially interventions for adolescents (a very under-developed field)

- the outcomes and broader impacts associated with the two fields in general and particular programmes and interventions within them

- the nature and impact of interventions that use only parenting support as compared with those that combine a range of family support. What is the evidence showing better outcomes? What are the relative achievements of approaches that combine a focus on parenting skills with interventions targeted at strengthening the capacity of the family to provide adequate care, to access basic social services, and to address barriers to social services and support?

- the extent to which a life course approach underpins the developments, barriers to its usage, and the potential of such an approach to transform family support and parenting support

- the factors making for or detracting from sustainability and scale-up, especially from a social and cultural viewpoint, and the impact of more formal types of support on existing informal support and family life and child-rearing generally

- the links between developments in family support and parenting support and other social policy goals and objectives. In particular, the extent to which the family support and parenting support measures are oriented to equality goals (such as those for gender, generation, race, ethnic group and religion) and how they interact with them (positively and negatively)

- the strengths and weaknesses of family support and parenting support in addressing problems that are structural in nature (e.g., poverty, inequality, unemployment, ill-health and poor education) and whether they represent a move away from unconditional and universal support for families, parents and children.

Source: Daly et al. (2015, pp.34–35)

CONCLUSION

Taking forward a global agenda for family support first requires recognition that there is a global responsibility for doing so by all those involved in whatever way within the field. There is a need for everyone engaging professionally with family support to make an effort to internationalise their work, recognising that they are part of an increasingly global workforce. With this goes the challenge to make sense of and respond proactively to the cross-national commonalities and differences. This involves critical reflection on developments that are occurring in services and programmes, and making judgements on how this is influencing the quality of practice – the responsibility to take a position.

Such active engagement with the globalisation of family support is necessary to help ensure that the changes that it is driving work for and not against families. The potential benefits for everyone involved – policy-makers, operational managers, practitioners, researchers and especially children, young people and their families – justifies the effort. Recognising and understanding the characteristics and processes of change captured in the concept of globalisation is essential if it is to be engaged with the interest of promoting family support. Ensuring the wellbeing and realising the potential of families will increasingly depend on sharing, debating and reflecting on diverse experience and understanding, so that international exchange becomes part of a growing global resource for family support.

Entering into the dialogue that international exchange involves requires being explicit about the positions that are being taken on family support and its various dimensions. This book has sought to argue for a perspective on family support expressed in an integrative definition:

> Family support is both a style of work and a set of activities; which reinforce positive informal social networks through integrated programmes; combining statutory, voluntary, community and private services, primarily focused on early intervention across a range of levels and needs with the aim of promoting and protecting the health, wellbeing and rights of all children, young people and their families in their own homes and communities, with particular attention to those who are vulnerable or at risk. (Dolan *et al.* 2006, p.16)

This definition, with its six components, is able to draw on the interlacing theories of social ecology, resilience, social capital and social support to provide the necessary framework for the reflective practice required to make the definition live. Realising the developmental view of family support that is the vision behind the definition requires application of the ten core practice principles. Practitioners of family support, whether delivering frontline services, managing those services, developing policy or undertaking research, must all ensure their practice strives to be child-centred, needs-led, strengths-based, socially inclusive, partnership-based, informal network-focused, easily accessed, responsive and flexible, collaborative in development and evidence-informed.

The developmental approach to family support being argued for cannot be achieved without a supportive, inclusive, mobilising politics in which the state is a driving force. There also has to be an organisational context in which the vision, the components of the definition and the practice principles are embedded. This will require learning organisations that are open and flatter, more collaborative and with a focus on identifying, managing and solving problems and generating new challenges within the solutions. Both politically and organisationally, family support requires an open systems perspective that recognises power, conflict and unintended consequences as a necessary part of the developmental dynamic.

At the heart of family support lies direct work with children, young people, parents and neighbourhoods. This is relational work in which the empowering quality of the encounter between those who provide and those who receive help and services is crucial. Resilience is both the goal and the means of achieving the desired outcomes of family support. A similar reframing of outcomes as the potential to be resourced and realised is central to the approach argued for in relation to evaluation and monitoring as an essential requirement. Rigorous, inclusive evaluation, theoretically informed and using advanced mixed methods, will make explicit and allow for the development of theories of change that explain logic models of impact as they apply to specific circumstances.

As noted at the very start of this book, having an explicit position on what family support is, should and could be is not about narrowing the concept, limiting it to a restricted set of practices, nor to quash debate. Rather, through arguing for an explicit position, the intention is to encourage others to do the same. In this way, the various options that exist can be made more open to examination and contest – not just as ideas, but also in practice. Taking and articulating clear positions provides a firmer basis for the work of all family support practitioners – frontline workers, managers, policy-makers, trainers and researchers. It provides the means for reflective practice not only to address the immediacy of practitioners' concerns, but also to make a contribution to the necessary global store of resources for developing future family support.

REFERENCES

Aarons, G.A., Green, A.E., Willging, C.E., Ehrhart, M.G. *et al.* (2014) 'Mixed-method study of a conceptual model of evidence-based intervention sustainment across multiple public-sector service settings.' *Implementation Science 9*, 183–195.

Adams, R. (2009) 'Being a Critical Practitioner.' In R. Adams, L. Dominelli and M. Payne (eds) *Critical Practice in Social Work* (2nd edn). Basingstoke: Palgrave Macmillan.

Allan, J. and Catts, R. (eds) (2012) *Social Capital, Children and Young People: Implications for Practice, Policy and Research.* Bristol: Policy Press.

Astbury, B. and Leeuw, F.L. (2010) 'Unpacking black boxes: mechanisms and theory building in evaluation.' *American Journal of Evaluation 31*, 3, 363–381.

Axford, B. (2013) *Theories of Globalization.* Cambridge: Polity Press.

Axford, N. (2013) 'Exploring the influence of international governmental organisations on domestic child welfare policy and practice.' *Adoption and Fostering 37*, 1, 57–70.

Barry, M. (2012) 'Social Capital in the Lives of Young Carers.' In J. Allan and R. Catts (eds) *Social Capital, Children and Young People.* Bristol: Policy Press.

Belsky, J., Melhuish, E., Barnes, J., Leyland, A.H. and Romaniuk, H. (2006) 'Effects of Sure Start local programmes on children and families: early findings from a quasi-experimental, cross sectional study.' *British Medical Journal 332*, 7556, 1476.

Beresford, P. (2005) 'Redistributing profit and loss: the new economics of the market and social welfare.' *Critical Social Policy 25*, 4, 464–482.

Bochel, C. and Bochel, H.M. (2004) *The UK Social Policy Process.* Basingstoke: Palgrave Macmillan.

Bolger, N. and Amarel, D. (2007) 'Effects of social support visibility on adjustment to stress: experimental evidence.' *Journal of Personality and Social Psychology 92*, 3, 458–475.

Bouckaert, G. and van Dooran, W. (2003) 'Performance Measurement and Management in Public Sector Organisations.' In T. Boivard and E. Loffler (eds) *Public Management and Governance*. London: Routledge.

Brady, B., Dolan, P. and Canavan, J. (2004) *Working for Children and Families: Exploring Good Practice*. Galway: Child & Family Research and Policy Unit, Western Health Board/National University of Ireland.

Broadhead, P., Meleady, C. and Delgado, M.A. (2008) *Children, Families and Communities: Creating and Sustaining Integrated Services*. Maidenhead: Open University Press.

Brofenbrenner, U. (1979) *The Ecology of Human Development*. Cambridge, MA: Harvard University Press.

Buckley, H., Carr, N. and Whelan, S. (2010) '"Like walking on eggshells": service user views and expectations of the child protection system.' *Child and Family Social Work 16*, 1, 101–110.

Callinicos, A. (1991) *Against Postmodernism: A Marxist Critique*. Cambridge: Polity Press.

Canavan, J. (2008) 'Resilience: cautiously welcoming a contested concept.' *Child Care in Practice 14*, 1, 1–7.

Canavan, J. (2010) 'Family support: policy, practice and research into the future.' *Administration 58*, 2, 15–32.

Canavan, J., Coen, L., Dolan, P. and Whyte, L. (2009) 'Privileging practice: facing the challenge of integrated working for outcomes for children.' *Children and Society 23*, 377–388.

Canavan, J., Dolan, P. and Pinkerton, J. (ed.) (2000) *Family Support: Direction from Diversity*. London: Jessica Kingsley Publishers.

Canavan, J., Dolan, P. and Pinkerton, J. (2003) 'Optimising the Relationships between Research, Policy and Practice: A Systemic Model.' In R. Munford and J. Sanders (eds) *Making a Difference in Families: Research that Creates Change*. New Zealand: Allen and Unwin Publishers.

Castro, F.G., Kellison, J.G., Boyd, S.J. and Kopak, A. (2010) 'A methodology for conducting integrative mixed methods research and data analyses.' *Journal of Mixed Methods Research 4*, 4, 342–360.

Cedara, B. and Levant, R.F. (1990) 'A meta-analysis of the effects of parent effectiveness training.' *The American Journal of Family Therapy 18*, 4, 373–384.

Chambers, D. (2012) *A Sociology of Family Life*. Cambridge: Polity Press.

Chief Secretary to the Treasury (2003) *Every Child Matters*. London: HMSO

Clarke, J., Bainton, D., Lendvai, N. and Stubbs, P. (2015) *Making Policy Move: Towards a Politics of Translation and Assemblage*. Bristol: Policy Press.

Cochrane, A. (1993) 'Comparative Approaches and Social Policy.' In A. Cochrane and J. Clarke (eds) *Comparing Welfare States*. London: Sage.

Connolly, M. and Masson, J. (2014) 'Private and public voices: does family group conferencing privilege the voice of children and families in child welfare?' *Journal of Social Welfare and Family Law 36*, 4, 403–414.

Creswell, J.W., Plano Clark, V.L., Gutmann, M.L. and Hanson, W.E. (2003) 'Advances in Mixed Methods Research Designs.' In A. Tashakkori and C. Teddlie (eds) *Handbook of Mixed Methods in Social and Behavioral Research*. Thousand Oaks, CA: Sage.

Cutrona, C.E. (2000) 'Social Support Principles for Strengthening Families.' In J. Canavan, P. Dolan and J. Pinkerton (eds) *Family Support: Direction from Diversity*. London: Jessica Kingsley Publishers.

Daly, M. (2011) *Welfare*. Cambridge: Polity Press.

Daly, M. and Kelly, G. (2015) *Families and Poverty: Everyday Life on a Low Income*. Bristol: Policy Press.

Daly, M. and Lewis, J. (2000) 'The concept of social care and the analysis of contemporary welfare states.' *British Journal of Sociology 51*, 2, 281–298.

Daly, M., Bray, R., Bruckauf, Z., Byrne, J. *et al.* (2015) *Family and Parenting Support: Policy and Provision in a Global Context*. Florence: UNICEF Office of Research.

Davis, J.M. (2011) *Integrated Children's Services*. London: Sage.

Davis, J.M. and Smith, M. (2012) *Working in Multi-professional Contexts: A Practical Guide for Professionals in Children's Services*. London: Sage.

Deacon, B. (2007) *Global Social Policy and Governance*. London: Sage.

Dermott, E. and Seymour, J. (2011) 'Developing "Displaying Families": A Possibility for the Future of the Sociology of Personal Life.' In E. Dermott and J. Seymour (eds) *Displaying Families: A New Concept for the Sociology of Family Life*. Basingstoke: Palgrave Macmillan.

Devaney, C. (2013) *An Evaluation of the Implementation of the Induction of Social Workers: A Policy and Guidelines for Children and Families Social Services*. Dublin: Child and Family Agency.

Devaney, C. and Dolan, P. (2014) 'Voice and meaning: the wisdom of family support veterans.' *Child and Family Social Work*. DOI: 10.1111/cfs.12200

Devaney, J. and Spratt, T. (2009) 'Child abuse as a complex and wicked problem: reflecting on policy developments in the United Kingdom in working with children and families with multiple problems.' *Children and Youth Services Review 31*, 6, 635–641.

DfES (Department for Education and Skills) (2004) *Every Child Matters*. Norwich: The Stationery Office.

Dill, K. and Shera, W. (2012) *Implementing Evidence-informed Practice: International Perspectives.* Toronto: Canadian Scholars Press.

Dolan, P. (2006) 'Assessment, Intervention and Self Appraisal Tools for Family Support.' In P. Dolan, J. Pinkerton and J. Canavan (eds) *Family Support as Reflective Practice.* London: Jessica Kingsley Publishers.

Dolan, P. (2008) 'Social support, social justice, and social capital: a tentative theoretical triad for community development.' *Community Development* 39, 1, 112–119.

Dolan, P. (2012) 'Travelling through Social Support and Youth Civic Action on a Journey towards Resilience.' In M. Ungar (ed.) *The Social Ecology of Resilience: A Handbook of Theory and Practice.* New York: Springer.

Dolan, P. and Brady, B. (2012) *A Guide to Youth Mentoring: Providing Effective Social Support.* London: Jessica Kingsley Publishers.

Dolan, P. and Canavan, J. (2000) 'Refocusing Project Work with Adolescents towards a Family Support Paradigm.' In J. Canavan, P. Dolan and J. Pinkerton (eds) *Family Support: Direction from Diversity.* London: Jessica Kingsley Publishers.

Dolan, P. and Cutrona, C. (2004) *The Adapted Social Provisions Scale.* Galway: Child and Family Research Centre, NUI Galway.

Dolan, P., Pinkerton, J. and Canavan, J. (2006) *Family Support as Reflective Practice.* London: Jessica Kingsley Publishers.

Eccles, M.P. and Mittman, B.S. (2006) 'Welcome to implementation science.' *Implementation Science 1*, 1.

Eyberg, S. and Pincus, D. (1999) *Eyberg Child Behavior Inventory and Sutter-Eyberg Student Behavior Inventory – Revised: Professional Manual.* Odessa, FL: Psychological Assessment Resources.

Featherstone, B. (2006) 'Rethinking family support in the current policy context.' *British Journal of Social Work 36*, 5–19.

Featherstone, B., White, S. and Morris, K. (2014) *Re-imagining Child Protection.* Bristol: Policy Press.

Ferguson, H. (2010) 'Walks, home visits and atmospheres: risk and the everyday practices and mobilities of social work and child protection.' *British Journal of Social Work 40*, 4, 1100–1117.

Fetterman, D.M. (2001) *Foundations of Empowerment Evaluation.* Thousand Oaks, CA: Sage.

Field, J. (2003) *Social Capital.* London: Routledge.

Finn, J.L., Nybell, L.M. and Shook, J.J. (2010) 'The meaning and making of childhood in the era of globalization: challenges for social work.' *Children and Youth Services Review 32*, 246–254.

Fixsen, D.L., Blase, K.A., Naoom, S.F. and Wallace, F. (2009) 'Core implementation components.' *Research on Social Work Practice 19*, 531–540.

Forde, C. (2015) 'Perspectives of Community Stakeholders.' In *Seen and Not Heard? The Lived Realities of Children and Young People's Participation in Ireland in Their Homes, Schools and Communities*. Dublin: Department of Children and Youth Affairs, Government of Ireland.

Friedman, M., Garnett, L. and Pinnock, M. (2005) 'Dude, Where's My Outcomes? Partnership Working and Outcome-based Accountability in the UK.' In J. Scott and H. Ward (eds) *Safeguarding and Promoting the Well-being of Children, Families and Communities*. London: Jessica Kingsley Publishers.

Frost, N. and Dolan, P. (2012) 'The Theoretical Foundations of Family Support Work.' In M. Davies (ed.) *Social Work with Children and Families*. London: Palgrave Macmillan.

Frost, N. and Stein, M. (1989) *The Politics of Child Welfare: Inequality, Power and Change*. Hemel Hempstead: Harvester/Wheatsheaf.

Frost, N., Abbott, S. and Race, T. (2015) *Family Support: Prevention, Early Intervention and Early Help*. Cambridge: Polity Press.

Gardner, R. (2003) 'A National Evaluation of Family Support Services: An Evaluation of Services Provided by the NSPCC in the United Kingdom.' In I. Katz and J. Pinkerton (eds) *Evaluating Family Support: Thinking Internationally, Thinking Critically*. Chichester: John Wiley & Sons.

Giddens, A. (1998) *The Third Way: The Renewal of Social Democracy*. Cambridge: Polity Press.

Gilligan, R. (2000) 'Family Support: Issues and Prospects.' In J. Canavan, P. Dolan and J. Pinkerton (eds) *Family Support: Directions from Diversity*. London: Jessica Kingsley Publishers.

Gilligan, R. (2008) 'Promoting resilience in young people in long term care – the relevance of roles and relationships in the domains of recreation and work.' *Journal of Social Work Practice 22*, 1, 37–50.

Gilligan, R. (2009a) *Promoting Resilience: Supporting Children and Young People Who Are in Care, Adopted or in Need*. London: British Agency for Adoption and Fostering.

Gilligan, R. (2009b) 'Positive Turning Points in the Dynamics of Change over the Life Course.' In J.A. Mancini and K.A. Roberto (eds) *Pathways of Human Development: Explorations of Change*. Baltimore, MD: Lexington Books.

Gillies, V. (2005) 'Meeting parents' needs? Discourses of "support" and "inclusion" in family policy.' *Critical Social Policy 25*, 1, 70–90.

Goodman, R. (1997) 'The Strengths and Difficulties Questionnaire: a research note.' *Journal of Child Psychology and Psychiatry 38*, 581–586.

Hardiker, P., Exton, K. and Barker, M. (1991) *Policies and Practices in Preventive Childcare.* Aldershot: Avebury.

Hawkins, J., Catalano, R., Arthur, M., Egan, E. *et al.* (2008) 'Testing communities that care: rationale and design of the community youth development study.' *Prevention Science 9*, 3, 178–190.

Heckman, J.J. (2006) 'Skill formation and the economics of investing in disadvantaged children.' *Science 312*, 5782, 1900–1902.

Hellinckx, W., Colton, M.J. and Williams, M. (1997) *International Perspectives on Family Support.* Aldershot: Arena.

Henderson, S., Holland, J., McGrellis, S., Sharpe, S. and Thomson, R. (2007) *Inventing Adulthoods: A Biographical Approach to Youth Transitions.* London: Sage.

Hendrick, H. (2003) *Child Welfare: Historical Dimensions, Contemporary Debate.* Bristol: Policy Press.

Hogan, C. (2001) *The Power of Outcomes: Strategic Thinking to Improve Results for Children, Families and Communities.* Available at www.conhogan.com/pdf/The-power-of-outcomes.pdf, accessed on 3 November 2008.

Howe, D. (1995) *Attachment Theory for Social Work Practice.* New York: Palgrave.

Jack, G. (1997) 'An ecological approach to social work with children and families.' *Child and Family Social Work 2*, 2, 109–120.

Jack, G. (2015) '"I may not know who I am, but I know where I am from": the meaning of place in social work with children and families.' *Child and Family Social Work 20*, 4, 415–423.

Jack, G. and Jordan, B. (1999) 'Social capital and child welfare.' *Children and Society 13*, 242–256.

Johnson, R.B., Onwuegbuzie, A.J. and Turner, L.A. (2007) 'Toward a definition of mixed methods research.' *Journal of Mixed Methods Research 1*, 2, 112–133.

Jones, R. (2015) 'The end game: the marketisation and privatisation of children's social work and child protection.' *Critical Social Policy 35*, 4, 447–469.

Jordan, B. and Drakeford, M. (2012) *Social Work and Social Policy under Austerity.* Basingstoke: Palgrave Macmillan.

Jordan, B. with Jordan, C. (2000) *Social Work and the Third Way: Tough Love as Social Policy.* London: Sage.

Kaplan, S.A. and Garrett, A.E. (2005) 'The use of logic models by community based initiatives.' *Evaluation and Programme Planning 28*, 2, 167–172.

Katz, I. and Pinkerton, J. (eds) (2003a) *Evaluating Family Support: Thinking Internationally, Thinking Critically.* Chichester: John Wiley & Sons.

Katz, I. and Pinkerton, J. (2003b) 'International Convergence and Divergence: Towards an Open System Model in the Evaluation of Family Support.' In I. Katz and J. Pinkerton (eds) *Evaluating Family Support: Thinking Internationally, Thinking Critically*. Chichester: John Wiley & Sons.

Kazi, M.A.F. (2003) *Realist Evaluation in Practice*. London: Sage.

Kazi, M.A.F., Pagkos, B. and Milch, H. (2011) 'Realist evaluation in wraparound: a new approach in social work evidence-based practice.' *Research on Social Work Practice 21*, 11, 75–84.

Kemmis, S., McTaggart, R. and Nixon, R. (2014) *The Action Research Planner: Doing Critical Participatory Action Research*. Singapore: Springer.

Kennan, D., Brady, B. and Forkan, C. (2016) *How Effective Are Structures and Procedures Intended to Support Children's Participation in Decision-Making in Child Welfare, Child Protection and Alternative Care Services? A Systematic Literature Review*. Galway/Dublin: UNESCO Child and Family Research Centre/Tusla.

Knott, C. and Scragg, T. (eds) (2010) *Reflective Practice in Social Work*. Transforming Social Work Practice Series. London: Learning Matters.

Krohn, J. (2015) 'Beyond outcome measures in child protection: using feedback to direct and evaluate social work practice.' *Practice 27*, 2, 79–95.

Leece, J. (2004) 'Money talks, but what does it say? Direct payments and the commodification of care.' *Practice 16*, 3, 211–221.

Lefevre, M. (2010) *Communicating with Children and Young People: Making a Difference*. Bristol: Policy Press.

Luthar, S., Cicchetti, D. and Becker, B. (2000) 'The construct of resilience: acritical evaluation and guidelines for future work.' *Child Development 71*, 3, 543–562.

Lyons, K., Manion, K. and Carlsen, M. (2006) *International Perspectives on Social Work: Global Conditions and Local Practice*. New York: Palgrave Macmillan.

Masten, A.S. (2014) *Ordinary Magic: Resilience in Development*. New York: The Guilford Press.

Midgley, J. (2004) 'The Complexities of Globalization: Challenges to Social Work.' In N.-T. Tan and A. Rowlands (eds) *Social Work around the World III: Globalization, Social Welfare and Social Work*. Berne: International Federation of Social Workers.

Millar, M. (2006) 'A Comparative Perspective: Exploring the Space for Family Support.' In P. Dolan, J. Pinkerton and J. Canavan (eds) *Family Support as Reflective Practice*. London: Jessica Kingsley Publishers.

Mills, M. (2014) 'Globalisation and Family Life.' In A. Abela and J. Walker (eds) *Contemporary Issues in Family Studies: Global Perspectives on Partnership, Parenting and Support in a Changing World*. Chichester: John Wiley & Sons.

Mishna, F. (2012) *Bullying: A Guide to Research, Intervention, and Prevention.* Oxford: Oxford University Press.

Mor Barak, M., Nissly, J. and Levin, A. (2001) 'Antecedents to retention and turnover among child welfare, social work, and other human service employees: what can we learn from past research? A review and meta-analysis.' *The Social Service Review 75*, 4, 625–661.

Moran, P., Ghate, D. and van der Merwe, A. (2004) *What Works in Parenting Support? A Review of the International Evidence.* Research Report 574. London: Policy Research Bureau.

Morris, K. (2012) 'Family Support: Policies for Practice.' In M. Davies (ed.) *Social Work with Children and Families.* New York: Palgrave Macmillan.

Morrison, T. (2000) *Supervision: An Action Learning Approach* (2nd edn). Brighton: Pavilion.

Morrison, T. (2009) *Guide to the Supervision of Newly Qualified Social Workers.* Leeds: Children's Workforce Development Council.

Mullender, A., Ward, D. and Fleming, J. (2013) *Empowerment in Action: Self-directed Groupwork.* Basingstoke: Palgrave Macmillan.

Munro, E., Taylor, J.S. and Bradbury-Jones, C. (2013) 'Understanding the causal pathways to child maltreatment: implications for health and social care policy and practice.' *Child Abuse Review 23*, 1, 61–74.

NESS (National Evaluation of Sure Start) Research Team (2004) 'The National Evaluation of Sure Start Local Programmes in England.' *Child and Adolescent Mental Health 9*, 2–8.

NESS (National Evaluation of Sure Start) Research Team (2010) *The Impact of Sure Start Local Programmes on Seven Year Olds and Their Families.* London: Department for Education.

Office of the First Minister and Deputy First Minister (2006) *Our Children and Young People – Our Pledge: A Ten Year Strategy for Children and Young People in Northern Ireland 2006–2016.* Belfast: Office of the First Minister and Deputy First Minister.

OMCYA (Office of the Minister for Children and Youth Affairs) (2007) *The Agenda for Children's Services: A Policy Handbook.* Dublin: OMCYA.

Ozan, J. (2014) 'Leadership in Theory-based Evaluation: An Exploration of the Feasibility and Added-value of Incorporating a Focus on Leadership in Programme Evaluation.' Unpublished doctoral thesis.

Palattiyil, G., Sidhva, D. and Chakrabarti, M. (eds) (2016) *Social Work in a Global Context: Issues and Challenges.* London: Routledge.

Parker, R. (1990) *Away from Home: A History of Child Care.* Ilford: Barnardo's.

Patel, L. (2005) *Social Welfare and Social Development in South Africa*. Cape Town: Oxford University Press Southern Africa.

Patton, M.Q. (2008) *Utilization-focused Evaluation*. Thousand Oaks, CA: Sage

Pawson, R. (2006) *Evidence-based Policy: A Realist Perspective*. Thousand Oaks, CA: Sage.

Payne, M. (2006) *What Is Professional Social Work?* Bristol: BASW/Policy Press.

Payne, M. and Askeland, G.A. (2008) *Globalization and International Social Work: Postmodern Change and Challenge*. Aldershot: Ashgate.

Petr, C.G. and Walter, U.M. (2005) 'Best practices inquiry: a multidimensional, value-critical framework.' *Journal of Social Work Education 41*, 251–267.

Pinkerton, J. (2006) 'The Irish National Children's Strategy: Lessons for Promoting the Social Inclusion of Children and Young People.' In E.K.M. Tisdall, J.M. Davis, M. Hill and A. Prout (eds) *Children, Young People and Social Inclusion: Participation for What?* Bristol: Policy Press.

Pinkerton, J. and Katz, I. (2003) 'Perspective through International Comparison in the Evaluation of Family Support.' In I. Katz and J. Pinkerton (eds) *Evaluating Family Support: Thinking Internationally, Thinking Critically.* Chichester: John Wiley & Sons.

Pinkerton, J., Higgins, K. and Devine, P. (2000) *Family Support – Linking Project Evaluation to Policy Analysis*. Aldershot: Ashgate.

Politt, C. and Bouckaert, G. (2004) *Public Management Reform: A Comparative Analysis*. Oxford: Oxford University Press.

Popple, K. (2015) *Analysing Community Work: Theory and Practice* (2nd edn). Maidenhead: Open University Press.

Powell, M. and Barrientos, A. (2011) 'An audit of the welfare modelling business.' *Social Policy and Administration 45*, 1, 69–84.

Redmond, S. and Dolan, P. (2014) 'Towards a conceptual model of youth leadership development.' *Child and Family Social Work*. DOI:10.111/cfs.12146

Ribbens McCarthy, J., Doolittle, M. and Day Sclater, S. (2008) *Family Meanings*. Milton Keynes: Open University Press.

Rossi, P., Lipsey, M. and Freeman, H. (2004) *Evaluation: A Systematic Approach*. Thousand Oaks, CA: Sage.

Ruch, G. (2007) 'Reflective practice in contemporary child-care social work: the role of containment.' *British Journal of Social Work 37*, 4, 659–680.

Ruch, G., Turney, D. and Ward, A. (2010) *Relationship-based Social Work*. London: Jessica Kingsley Publishers.

Rutter, M. (2012) 'Resilience: Causal Pathways and Social Ecology.' In M. Ungar (ed.) *The Social Ecology of Resilience: A Handbook of Theory and Practice*. New York, NY: Springer-Verlag.

Sackett, D.L., Rosenberg, W.M.C., Gray, J.A.M., Haynes, R.B. and Richardson, W.S. (1996) 'Evidence based medicine: what it is and what it isn't.' *British Medical Journal 312*, 71–72.

Sanders, M.R. (2012) 'Development, evaluation, and multinational dissemination of the Triple P-Positive Parenting Program.' *Annual Review of Clinical Psychology 8*, 345–379.

Sassen, S. (2007) *A Sociology of Globalization*. New York: W.W. Norton.

Schwandt, T.A. (2005) 'The centrality of practice to evaluation.' *American Journal of Evaluation 26*, 1, 95–105.

Sewpaul, V. (2004) 'Globalization, African Governance and the New Partnership for Africa's Development.' In N.-T. Tan and A. Rowlands (eds) *Social Work around the World III: Globalization, Social Welfare and Social Work*. Berne: International Federation of Social Workers.

Shaw, A., Brady, B., McGrath, B., Brennan, M. and Dolan, P. (2014) 'Understanding youth civic engagement: debates, discourses and lessons from practice.' *Community Development 45*, 4, 300–316.

Smith, R. (2008) *Social Work and Power*. Basingstoke: Palgrave Macmillan.

Spratt, T. (2009) 'Identifying families with multiple problems: possible responses from child and family social work to current policy developments.' *British Journal of Social Work 39*, 3, 435–450.

Stafford, A., Parton, N., Vincent, S. and Smith, C. (2012) *Child Protection Systems in the United Kingdom: A Comparative Analysis*. London: Jessica Kingsley Publishers.

Statham, J. and Smith, M. (2010) *Issues in Early Intervention: Identifying and Supporting Children with Additional Needs*. London: Department for Children, Schools and Families.

Thomas, N. and Percy-Smith, B. (2012) '"It's about changing services and building relationships": evaluating the development of Children in Care Councils.' *Child and Family Social Work 17*, 487–496.

Thompson, N. (2008) 'Focusing on outcomes: developing systematic practice.' *Practice 20*, 1, 5–16.

Thompson, N. (2009) *People Skills* (3rd edn). Basingstoke: Palgrave Macmillan.

Thompson, N. (2012) *Anti-discriminatory Practice* (5th edn). Basingstoke: Palgrave Macmillan.

Thompson, R.A. (2015) 'Social support and child protection: lessons learned and learning.' *Child Abuse and Neglect 41*, 19–29.

UN (United Nations) (1989) *Convention on the Rights of the Child*. Geneva: UN.

Ungar, M. (2008) 'Resilience across cultures.' *British Journal of Social Work 38*, 2, 218–235.

Ungar, M. (2012) *The Social Ecology of Resilience: A Handbook of Theory and Practice*. New York: Springer.

Ungar, M., Brown, M., Liebenberg, L., Othman, R. *et al.* (2007) 'Unique pathways to resilience across cultures.' *Adolescence 42*, 166, 287–310.

Webster-Stratton, C. and Reid, M.J. (2010) 'Adapting the Incredible Years, an evidence-based programme, for families involved in the child welfare system.' *Journal of Children's Services 5*, 25–42.

Weiss, C. (1995) 'Nothing as Practical as Good Theory: Exploring Theory-based Evaluation for Comprehensive Community Initiatives for Children and Families.' In J. Connell, A.C. Kubisch, L.B. Schorr and C.H. Weiss (eds) *New Approaches to Evaluating Community Initiatives: Concepts, Methods, and Contexts*. Washington, DC: Aspen Institute.

Welbourne, P. (2012) *Social Work with Children and Families: Developing Advanced Practice*. Abingdon: Routledge.

Welbourne, P. and Dixon, J. (2013) *Child Protection and Child Welfare: A Global Appraisal of Cultures, Policy and Practice*. London: Jessica Kingsley Publishers.

Wells, K. (2009) *Childhood in a Global Perspective*. Cambridge: Polity Press.

Whittaker, J.K. (2009) 'Evidence-based intervention and services for high-risk youth: a North American perspective on the challenges of integration for policy practice and research.' *Child and Family Social Work 14*, 2, 166–177.

Whittaker, J.K. and Garbarino, J. (1983) *Social Support Networks: Informal Helping in the Human Services*. New York: Aldine de Gruyter.

Williams, C. and Graham, M. (2014) 'A world on the move: migration, mobilities and social work.' *British Journal of Social Work 44*, suppl. 1, June, i1–i17.

Williams, P. (2002) 'The competent boundary spanner.' *Public Administration 80*, 103–124.

Williams, P. (2010) 'Special Agents: The Nature and Role of Boundary Spanners.' Presentation at the ESRC Seminar Series on 'Collaborative Futures: New Insights from Intra and Inter-Sectoral Collaborations', University of Birmingham, February.

Williams, P. (2013) 'We are all boundary spanners now?' *International Journal of Public Sector Management 26*, 1, 17–32.

Wilson, G. (2013) 'Evidencing reflective practice in social work education: theoretical uncertainties and practical challenges.' *British Journal of Social Work 43*, 1, 154–172.

Winter, K. (2011) *Building Relationships and Communicating with Young Children: A Practical Guide for Social Workers.* Abingdon: Routledge.

World Bank (2015) *Ending Extreme Poverty and Sharing Prosperity: Progress and Policies.* Washington, DC: World Bank.

Yeates, N. (2001) *Globalization and Social Policy.* London: Sage.

Yeates, N. (ed.) (2014) *Understanding Global Social Policy* (2nd edn). Bristol: Policy Press.

Yeates, N. (2015) *A Hundred Key Questions for the Post-2015 Development Agenda.* United Nations Research Institute for Social development – Sheffield Institute for International Development, Palais des Nations.

SUBJECT INDEX

AUTHOR INDEX